ALIEN ENCYCLOPAEDIA

MICHAEL JOHNSTONE

Published in Great Britain in 1998
by Madcap Books,
André Deutsch Ltd, 76 Dean Street, London, W1V 5HA
André Deutsch is a subsidiary of VCI plc
HYPERLINK http://www.vci.co.uk

Copyright © 1998 Madcap Books

The right of Michael Johnstone to be identified as the author of this work has been asserted by him in accordance with the Copyright, Designs and Patents Act, 1988

A catalogue record for this book is available from the British Library

ISBN 0 233 99236 7

All rights reserved. This book is sold subject to the condition that it may not be reproduced, stored in a retrieval system, or transmitted in any form or by any means, electronic, mechanical, photocopying, recording or otherwise, without the publisher's prior consent.

Printed in Great Britain

INTRODUCTION

Welcome to a world where
strange things happen.
A world where shining objects appear in
the sky, hover briefly, then zoom off in a
dazzling flash of light.
A world where curious craft land and
are seen and wondered at by a mere
handful
of men and women.
A world where strange humanoid
creatures step out from these craft.
A world where ordinary people are
whisked into space and later returned
to tell their stories to a disbelieving
audience.
Welcome to the world of UFOs.
Welcome to The Spook Files
Encyclopaedia of Aliens.

IN THE BEGINNING BC

UFOs and alien landings did not begin in the twentieth century – nor the nineteenth – nor the eighteenth. Let's go back to the beginning, to the very first recorded sightings . . .

EGYPT 1500 BC

'In the year 22 in the third month of the winter, the sixth hour of the day, there was a circle of fire coming from the sky.' That's what is written on a papyrus found in the Vatican. The scribe went on to describe the alien creature that appeared. It was headless, and gave out a foul odour. Its body was five metres wide and five metres long. It wasn't alone. A few days later fiery circles filled the sky and outshone the sun.

The Pharaoh himself, Thutmose III, left his palace and, accompanied by soldiers, went to witness the UFOs. 'Thereupon,' the scribe writes, 'these fire circles ascended higher in the sky towards the south . . .'

IRAQ 600BC

The prophet Ezekiel was astonished when he saw a great whirlwind come out of the north and from its midst stepped four creatures with four heads and four wings apiece. One of their four faces was that of a man, another the face of a lion, the third of an ox and the fourth of an eagle. The aliens 'sparkled like the colour of burnished brass.'

As he watched, a wheel within a wheel appeared, hovered in the air, then shot heavenward, taking all the creatures with it.

Had Ezekiel just had a close encounter of the Biblical type?

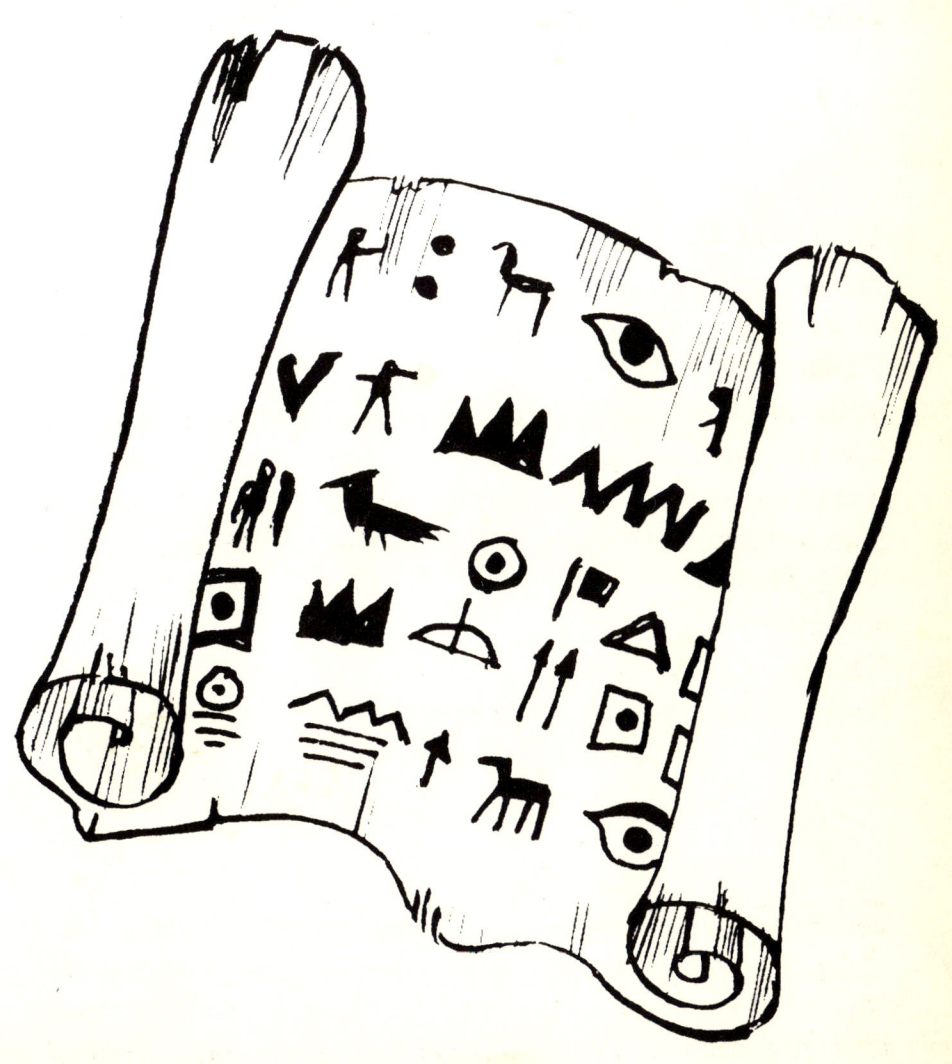

SPOOK FILES ENCYCLOPAEDIA

RIVER JORDAN 900BC

According to the Bible in the Second Book of Kings, after Elijah and his son Elisha had crossed the Jordan, they were just talking together when suddenly a chariot of fire drawn by fiery horses appeared from nowhere and parted the two of them. Elisha watched in astonishment as his dad, Elijah, was swept up by a whirlwind into heaven.

A miracle, or the first recorded case of Alien Abduction?

SPOOK FILES ENCYCLOPAEDIA

NEWSFLASH • NEWSFLASH • NEWSFLASH
ALEXANDER THE GREAT AIDED BY ALIENS

Tyre *332BC*
Reports have just come through that during the siege of Tyre, Lebanese and Macedonian troops saw UFOs flying over the besieged city. An eyewitness described the four small shields flying in triangular formation around a larger, central one.

As the troops watched, a beam of light shot from the largest UFO and struck the city wall, leaving a gaping hole in it. Alexander's men were quick to take advantage and streamed into the city, which was soon theirs.

ROME 213BC and 203BC

Writing around the time of the birth of Christ, Livy, the famous Roman historian, tells the story of a UFO that had been seen at Hadria, near Venice in Italy. It was described as 'an altar in the sky surrounded by men in white'. Ten years after that sighting, according to Julius Obsequens, another distinguished man of Rome, a dazzling torch streaked ugh the sky, from the west to the east, over Setie, not far ꜜpital. It was accompanied by what he could only nother object.'

INTO ALIEN DOMAIN

Let's leave the Romans behind and step into more modern times. Well, not exactly modern. AD 793 to be precise, when 'Fiery dragons in the sky alarmed the wretched nation of the English.'

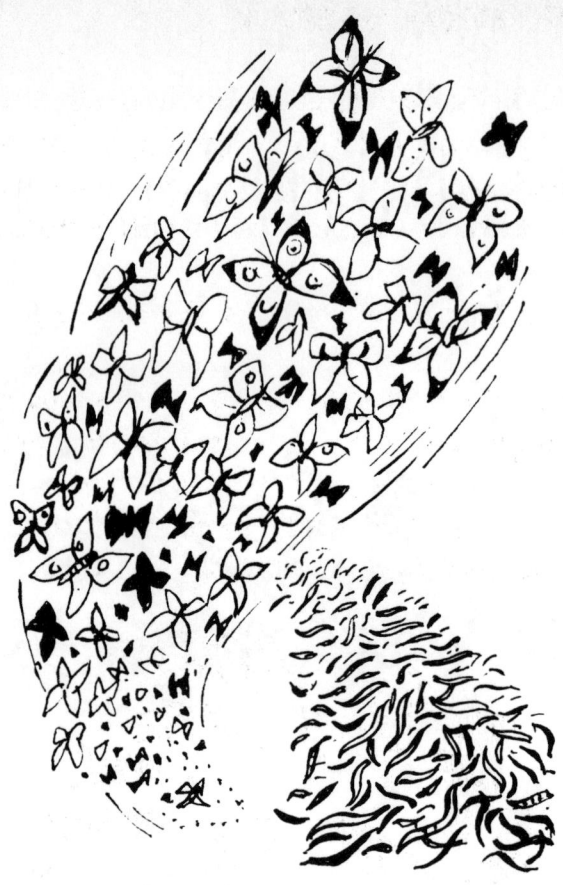

Then step forward to 1104 in Switzerland where . . . 'There were, near the stars, what looked like swarms of butterflies and little fiery worms of a strange kind. They flew in the air and took away the light of the Sun, just as if they had been clouds.'

Seven years later a group of pilgrims from Laon in France crossed the Channel into Wessex, carrying with them relics which they claimed were of the Virgin Mary. The saintly churchmen used these relics to heal the men and women stricken by 'incurable' illness. As they made their way along the south coast of England, sick people flocked to them. But when they arrived at Christchurch in Hampshire, their work was interrupted by a fire-breathing monster from the sea.

SIX OF THE BEST

1. 'A great star like a torch appeared in the south and climbed up into the sky, giving out a great light. It was shaped like a great head, back and front, and poured out smoke and flashes. It then turned towards the north, as if it wished to ascend to a place in the air.'
Matthew Paris, Chronicler of St Albans, England, 1239

2. 'There was a fire in the sky, like a burning and revolving wheel, or a round barrel of flame, emitting fire from above, and others in the shape of a long fiery beam were seen through a great deal of the winter in the county of Leicester.'
Henry Knighton, Leicester, England, 1388

3. 'The object that appeared in the night sky was as long and wide as a half-moon. It hung stationary for about a quarter of an hour, then suddenly spiralled, twisted and turned like a spring and rose up into heaven.'
The Duke of Burgogne, Reims, France, 1461

4. 'A strange and cruel sight was seen in the sky. The cross was yellow in colour and fearful to behold.'
Lycosthenes, Utrecht, Holland, 1528

5. 'Black spheres appeared at sunrise. Many became red and fiery, ending by being consumed and vanishing.'
Samuel Coccius, Basel, Switzerland, 1566

6. 'Out of the cloud came forth large, tall and wide objects like hats, and the Earth showed itself yellow and bloody, and seemed to be covered with hats.'
Pierre Boaistou, Tubingen, Germany, 1577

EYEWITNESS

It happened one evening in August 1972 while Norma Hissong, a young American housewife, was out driving with her husband and six-year-old daughter, Dawna, who was in the back seat. As they passed a store in Burlington, Massachusetts, they spotted an old friend they hadn't seen for some time so they pulled into the parking lot alongside her car and got out to have a chat, leaving Dawna in their car.

Suddenly Dawna leaned out the window and said, 'Look! It's a flying saucer.'

Naturally everyone thought she was pulling their legs, trying to get attention, so they just ignored her and carried on talking. But she wouldn't stop hollering, 'Look! It's a flying saucer.'

Eventually Norma's husband, Jack, turned to her and said, 'That's not a flying saucer, it's a . . .' and looking at where she was pointing, gasped, 'FLYING SAUCER!'

Everyone gazed upwards and there, suspended in the sky above them, was a huge disc-shaped object shimmering with light. 'Time,' Norma said later, 'seemed to stand still as we stared at it.'

Suddenly they heard the roar of an approaching airplane, probably, they thought, from Bedford Air Base in the next town. The flying saucer zoomed off at astonishing speed and vanished in the blink of an eye.

Norma and her husband jumped into the car and headed off in the direction the UFO had taken, hoping to catch a glimpse of it again. But the sky was clear.

As they slowed down, to turn to head for home, they saw three or four young men standing beside a car, obviously excited about something.

'What's the matter?' Norma's husband asked, drawing up beside them.

'We've just seen a . . . a UFO,' gasped one of them.

'So have we,' Norma said, leaning across Jack.

'Thank goodness for that,' said another of the boys. 'We thought we must have been hallucinating!'

When Norma and her family got home they called the air base at Bedford to tell them what they had seen. 'It was nothing,' the officer Norma spoke to assured her. 'It was just one of our aircraft towing something.'

She didn't really believe him but realized it was pointless arguing.

Then, nineteen years later, almost to the day, she saw a video on a television show about UFOs, shot in Colorado. The flying saucer that had been caught on camera was almost identical to the one the Hissongs had seen at Burlington – same shape, same shimmering lights – and Norma is now certain that what she encountered in 1976 was no 'aircraft towing something.' It was definitely a UFO.

Two aliens landed in the countryside miles from anywhere. They left their flying saucer to stroll along a country lane.

When they approached a red letter box, one of the aliens stopped and said, 'Take me to your leader.'

'Don't be silly,' said the second alien. 'It's only a baby!'

DENISON DAILY NEWS
January 25, 1878

A STRANGE PHENOMENON

Mr John Martin, a farmer who lives some six miles north of this city, was out hunting when his attention was directed to a dark object in the northern sky.

The peculiar shape and velocity with which the object seemed to approach riveted his attention, and he strained his eyes to discover its character. When first noticed, it appeared to be about as big as an orange, after which it continued to grow in size.

After gazing at it for some time, Mr Martin became blind from such long looking, and left off viewing to rest his eyes. On resuming his watch, the object was almost overhead, had increased considerably in size and appeared to be going through space at a wonderful speed. When directly over him, the object was the size of a large saucer.

And that's how the phrase FLYING SAUCER was born.

INTO THE TWENTIETH CENTURY

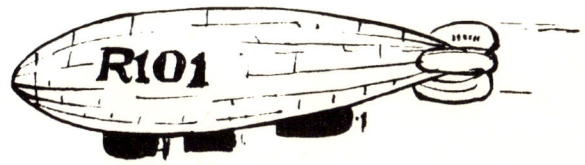

The twentieth century saw the birth of the airship and aircraft industries, and as the number of aircraft increased, so did the number of UFO sightings!

But no aeroplane was reported missing over the Irish Sea when one night in 1922 the coxswain of a Welsh lifeboat saw what looked like an aircraft descending slowly into the sea. And there was no sign of debris when he and another witness launched the boat to look for survivors.

No plane matches the description of a UFO given by American author Ella Young as she sat outside a Californian hotel. The cigar-shaped craft 'shot out of a cloud beyond the bay and across the sky toward Tamalais. It was long and slender, yellow and travelling at great speed.' Even more curiously, it moved like a worm, alternately 'contracting and elongating its body.'

No one else saw the light travelling at 160 km/h (100 mph) off the coast of Virginia one night in August 1929. But Tom Stuart, the mate on the SS Coldwater, swore he had seen a large passenger aircraft and was so vehement in his assertion that the coastguard checked with every airline and with the United States Air Force. There were no planes reported in the area!

There were plenty of planes in the skies during World War II (1939-1945). And several pilots had a close encounter of the first kind (see page 00) with what became known as the Foo Fighters – balls of fire – some only a few centimetres across, but others ten times that size.

Pilots assumed they were enemy inventions, designed either to scare them or take photographs of the area below. But pilots on both sides saw the Foo Fighters, and no country, Allies or Axis, has ever admitted to putting them into the air.

Foo Fighters were seen in many places, including:

Burma, 1943: Flying from Burma to China, US bomber pilots were buzzed by Foo Fighters and their instruments failed to function until the FFs backed off.

Germany, 1943: B-17 pilots belonging to US 348th Bomb Group were about to swing into action when they flew into hundreds of FFs heading in their direction. One pilot claimed his plane had been hit by an FF, which bounced harmlessly off his tail and then vanished at speed.

Germany, 1944: Night-fighter pilot David McFalls saw two FFs – 'huge, bright orange lights' as he described them – closing in on him. McFalls lost height and then banked his plane, but the FF stayed with him before heading off in the opposite direction.

Sumatra, 1944: Flying at 4,200 metres (14,000 feet) at about 340 km/h (210 mph) on a mission from India to bomb Japanese fortifications on the island, the co-pilot and a gunner of a plane reported to the pilot that an FF was flying alongside. Alvah Reida, the pilot, did everything he could to shake off their unwanted compan-ion, but the FF stayed in position for eight minutes before suddenly zooming off at right angles and quickly vanishing.

Were FFs just light reflected from tiny ice crystals?
Ball lightning?
Some other natural phenomenon? Or UFOS?

SPOOK FILES ENCYCLOPAEDIA

NEWSFLASH APRIL 1947!

While tracking a weather balloon over Richmond, Virginia, late this afternoon, Walter A Miczewski and other members of the US Weather Bureau claimed they saw a silver flat-bottomed disc with a dome on the top. They watched it for fifteen seconds before it vanished.

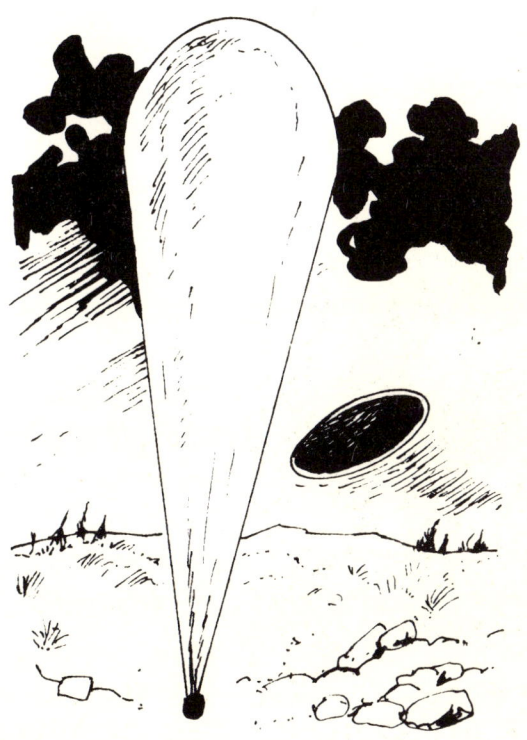

Miczewski wasn't the first to see what Ufologists call Daylight Discs. A few days before, one was spotted flying at a low altitude over Col de Serres in France. And April, May and June turned out to be a bumper month for UFO spotters as the following diary extract shows.

MAY 1947
12 Monday
Small silvery object fell out of the sky and crumbled over Washington State.

19 Monday
Cigar-shaped object spotted flying at speed at sunset in Richmond, Virginia.

20 Tuesday
Silvery object hovered over Manitou Springs, Colorado, then performed dazzling display of aerial acrobatics before rising and flying out of sight.

JUNE 1947
10 Monday
Ten-second sighting over Arizona of curious light that changed shape before vanishing in the blink of an eye.

Fifty Hungarian men and women reported seeing silvery balls zooming across the sky at breathtaking speed.

17 Monday
Ten UFOs spotted over California. Thirty metres (100 feet) in diameter, they travelled at 1000 km/h (600 mph).

24 Monday
Eight house-sized discs seen floating in the sky in Washington and landing somewhere in Idaho.

Six huge 'washtubs' flying in formation at amazing speed over Yukon, Oklahoma.

IN THEIR OWN WORDS

'I was pilot of the plane when we saw the UFO. We were flying in a Cessna Citation at maybe nine or ten o'clock at night. We were near Bakersfield when the Governor and the others called my attention to a big light flying a bit behind my plane. It appeared to be several hundred metres away. It was a fairly steady light until it began to accelerate, then it appeared to elongate. Then the light took off. It went up at a 45-degree angle, from a normal cruise speed to a fantastic speed instantly.'

BILL PAYTNER (PILOT)

What Bill Paytner saw was confirmed by one of the passengers aboard the Cessna.

'We followed it for several minutes. All of a sudden, to our utter amazement, it went straight up into the heavens. When I got off the plane I told Nancy all about it. And we read up on the long history of UFOs.'

GOVERNOR (LATER PRESIDENT) RONALD REAGAN

Tacoma,
Puget Sound,
Washington State.
Summer, 1947

Dear Mom,

I just had to tell you what's been happening here since Summer Camp started. It's like something from the movies.

Two or three weeks ago, June 21, I think it was, one of the coastguards, Harry Dahl, his fifteen-year-old boy, his dog and another coastguard (don't know his name) were patrolling the Sound. It was a bleak, cloudy day, and at about 2.00 p.m. they anchored just off Maury Island, about three miles from Tacoma.

Something made them look up, they don't know what. But when they did, they almost fell overboard when they saw six large doughnut-shaped objects hovering noiselessly in the sky.

As they stared, five of the UFOs (it means

Unidentified Flying Object, Mom) began to circle round the sixth, which then began to sink towards the water. Mr Dahl reckons it was 100 feet (if you are talking to any of your French cousins and tell them about this, say it was 30 metres – the French and other Europeans don't understand our way of measuring things) and it had a hole in the middle about 25 feet (8 metres) across.

Around the rim there were portholes about 6 feet (2 metres) in diameter and above them round windows fitted with dark glass.

Mr Dahl was terrified as it looked like the UFO was about to crash into the boat, so he pulled it onto the beach, grabbed his camera and stood on the sand taking photographs.

Unfortunately he ran out of film just as the middle UFO began to pour molten metal into the water and along the shore.

Mom, it killed the dog and injured the Dahl boy. Then it rose back to join the others and shot away across the Pacific.

The metal was still scalding hot, but Mr Dahl managed to scoop up samples on a stone, pushed his boat back into the water, and headed for home.

As soon as they were back in harbour, Mr Dahl told Fred Crisman what had happened. (Mr Crisman's his superior officer).

Mom, the next bit's even spookier.

The next morning a man wearing a dark suit turned up at the Dahls in a big black sedan. He told him he knew what had happened and that he'd best not tell anyone if he knew what was good for his family.

The day after that, Fred Crisman went to the island to see if he could find any of the bits of metal, which would have cooled and hardened by then. While he was looking, another UFO appeared, scudded across the bay, then disappeared.

When he got back, he developed the photographs Mr. Dahl had taken, but they were covered in white spots as

though they had been damaged by radiation.
    Isn't that a blast?
    Your loving son,
    Ben.

Apartment 45, 70 West Street,
New York, NY 20011
August 1987

Dear Ben,

    I was cleaning out a closet last week when I came across a letter you wrote to Mom, the year you were at Summer Camp at Washington and someone there claimed to have seen a UFO.

    It was a real coincidence, because I'd just been reading an article by someone called John Keel, who's some sort of expert in UFOs. Apparently the whole Maury Island affair was a great hoax!

    You remember how the Maury Island thing was happening around the same time as Ken Arnold saw a flying saucer in Washington [see page 42]. Well, he heard what had happened at Maury Sound and contacted Fred Crisman. Later he talked to a Lieut. Brown at a California army base and asked him to help with the investigation. Brown and another man called Davidson hopped on a B-42 bomber and flew up to Washington to talk to Crisman.

Lieut. Brown didn't have time to visit the island, but he took away a large box of the metal chips before heading back to California.

Next day Crisman phoned Arnold with the news that the B-42 had crashed, after one of the engines had caught fire. Brown and Davidson were both dead.

He told Arnold to come to the Sound so that they could both go to the island. But for some reason the boat's engines wouldn't start.

Crisman said he'd call Arnold at his hotel room as soon as it was fixed. He never did.

He said he'd send over the photographs. He never did.

When Arnold tried to contact him, he'd disappeared.

A few days later, Dahl's son disappeared.

Then Arnold found out that his hotel room was being bugged, so he hot footed it out of town, convinced someone didn't want the Maury Island affair to be investigated.

BUT, this John Keel guy has come up with another version. Crisman had been in cahoots for years with a sci-fi magazine and when he read about the Ken Arnold UFO, he decided to climb on the bandwagon. So, with the help of Dahl, he dreamed up the story and tried to sell it to the mag.

When Brown and Davidson talked to Crisman, they could see right away that he was a fraud. He wasn't even a coastguard. (You weren't to know that. You were just visiting the area.) Neither was Dahl.

Thinking they'd be blamed for the B-42 crash, both men went walkabout, as they say in Australia.

BUT apparently the two men DID see something on the Sound that day. A couple of planes were flying over the area when one of them got into trouble and began dumping radioactive slag, thinking it would just fall into the water. Unfortunately, some fell on the boat, killing Dahl's dog and injuring his son.

The Dahl boy hadn't disappeared as Arnold thought. He was in hospital!

Oh, there was a Man in Black, though – a security agent from the Atomic Energy Commission who traced Dahl through the hospital records!

Sorry to spoil your story after all those years.

Your loving sister,

Mary Beth.

So, one of the most famous UFO sightings of the 1940s turned out to be a hoax. But never mind, for we are about to enter the next era of the UFO story – and this one opens almost exactly where the previous one stopped – in June 1947, when a routine flight over the Cascade Mountains in Washington State gave birth to a veritable cascade of UFO sightings.

But before we look at many of these, it's time for . . .

EYEWITNESS

For many years I have lived with a secret, in a secrecy imposed on all specialists in astronautics. I can now reveal that every day in the USA, our radar instruments capture objects of form and composition unknown to us. And there are thousands of witness reports and a quantity of documents to prove this, but nobody wants to make them public. Why? Because the authorities are afraid that people may think of all kinds of horrible invaders. So the password still is, "we have to avoid panic by all means."

I was, furthermore, a witness to an extraordinary phenomenon on the planet Earth. It happened in Florida. There I saw with my own eyes a defined area of ground being consumed with flames, with four indentations left by a flying object which had descended in the middle of a field. Beings had left this craft (there were other traces to prove this). They seemed to have studied topography, they had collected soil samples and eventually they returned to where they had come from, disappearing at enormous speed.

I happen to know that the authorities did just about everything to keep this incident from the press and TV, in fear of a panicky reaction from the public.'

These, it is said, are the words of Major Gordon Cooper, one of the United States' most famous astronauts and not the only American 'spaceman' who claims to have seen a UFO.

In 1951, when he was flying his jet fighter over West Germany, two saucer-shaped discs appeared high above him, giving him a barn-storming display of aerial acrobatics. As he later testified before an official committee, 'I believe that these extraterrestrial vehicles and their crews are visiting this planet from other planets, and that most astronauts are reluctant to discuss UFOs. I did have occasion in 1951 to have two days of observation of many flights of them, of different sizes flying in fighter formation, generally from east to west over Europe.'

Twelve years later, during the final stages of a twenty-two orbit flight in his Mercury capsule, Cooper saw a glowing green object zooming towards his spacecraft. He immediately reported what he had seen to a tracking station in Australia where radar tracked the object.

Cooper's report was picked up by an American television station which was following every stage of the mission, but when Cooper returned to Earth, the station's newsmen had been warned by the US government not to ask him about what they had heard.

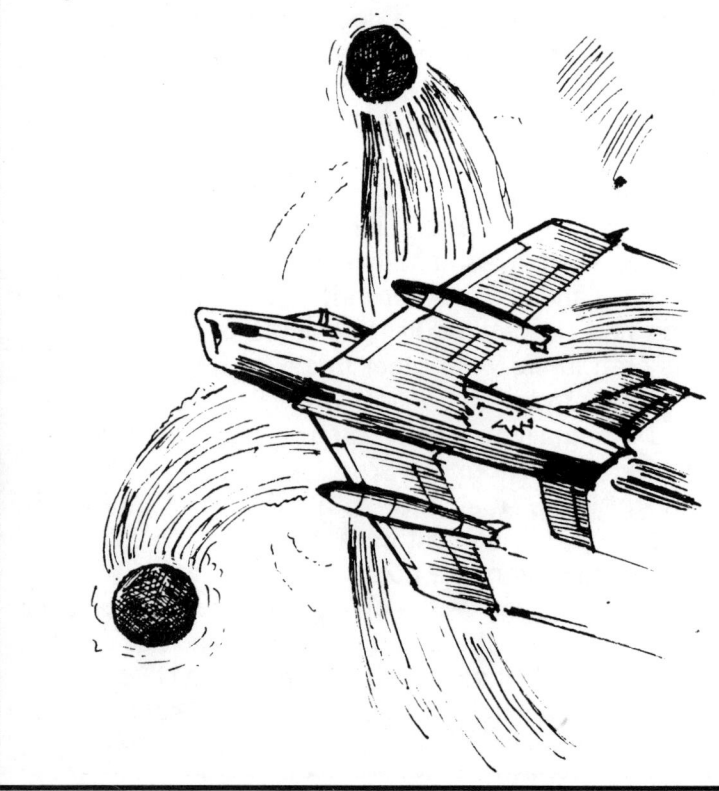

STOP PRESS STOP PRESS STOP PRESS

ALIEN MOVIE SMASHES BOX OFFICE RECORDS

December 1989:

Stephen Spielberg's film, ET: THE EXTRATERRESTRIAL, has become the biggest movie earner in Hollywood History. Including sales of the video, the movie has earned $700 million!

STOP PRESS STOP PRESS STOP PRESS

CLOSE ENCOUNTERS 1-5

Dr J Allen Hynek is one of the world's leading UFO experts or, to give them their proper name, ufologists. He has classified UFO and alien sightings into what he calls Close Encounters.

Close Encounters of the First Kind: occur when UFOs are seen at close quarters. This is the most common kind of encounter.

Close Encounters of the Second Kind: happen when a UFO is not just seen but leaves traces of itself behind. Anyone who has ever seen a corn circle – one of those elaborate circular patterns that appear in the middle of a cornfield with no hint of how it got there – may have had had a close encounter of the first kind – had they got there a few hours earlier!

Close Encounters of the Third Kind: take place when someone actually sees the crew of a UFO, or in other words, sees an alien or aliens. Probably the best known close encounter of the third kind occurs in the film of the same name.

Two more kinds of close encounters have been added to Dr Hynek's original list.

Close Encounters of the Fourth Kind: are also known as alien abductions. They occur when someone is taken by aliens into their UFO or into another time/space dimension.

Close Encounters of the Fifth Kind: this is when a human being is contacted by aliens through telepathic communication.

SPOOK FILES ENCYCLOPAEDIA

DISTANT SIGHTINGS

Close Encounters are one of two categories of UFO sightings, according to Dr Hynek. The other is Distant Sightings.

An Encounter has to take place within 150 metres (500 feet) of a witness to qualify as 'Close'. UFO sightings beyond that are known as 'Distant Sightings'. Dr Hynek placed them in three categories.

Daylight Discs are flying objects of various shapes and sizes – boomerang, cigar, egg, sphere or triangle – and are seen during the day.

Nocturnal Lights are seen after dark and count as UFO sightings only after investigation has shown that their lights were not from conventional aircraft or caused by natural phenomena, such as shooting stars or volcanic debris.

Radar-visuals occur when an eyewitness account is backed up by a recording on a scientific instrument such as a radar screen.

DAYLIGHT DISCS

Washington State – June 24, 1947: this is the sighting that launched the modern UFO age. Earlier in the month, a US Marine Corps C-46 went down in Washington's Cascade Mountains with 32 men on board. A 5,000 dollar reward was offered to anyone who spotted the plane.

An experienced pilot, Ken Arnold, had a few hours to spare so he took off to join the search in his single-engine Callier, a plane specially designed for flying over mountains and capable of landing on rough ground.

As he flew at 3,000 metres (9,200 feet) a huge flash of light bathed his aircraft. In the distance he saw a DC-4, but it was too far away to have caused the flash. Suddenly, a second flash hit his plane. Arnold looked around and, in his own words, saw, 'far to my left and to the north, a formation of very bright objects coming from the vicinity of Mount Baker, flying very close to the mountain tops at tremendous speed.'

Arnold calculated from the speed of his own plane that the nine crescent-shaped aircraft he was watching must have been travelling at 2750 km/h (1700 mph). In 1947, nothing could fly at that speed.

'They didn't fly like ordinary aircraft,' Arnold said later. 'They flew in formation, but erratically, like speedboats on rough water, or like the tail of a Chinese kite blowing in the wind. Maybe it would be best to describe them as very similar to a flight of geese in a rather diagonal chain-like line, as if they were linked together. And as they flew, they flashed blue and white.'

As soon as they were out of sight, he called off his search for the missing plane and headed back to base, 'to tell some of the boys what I had seen.'

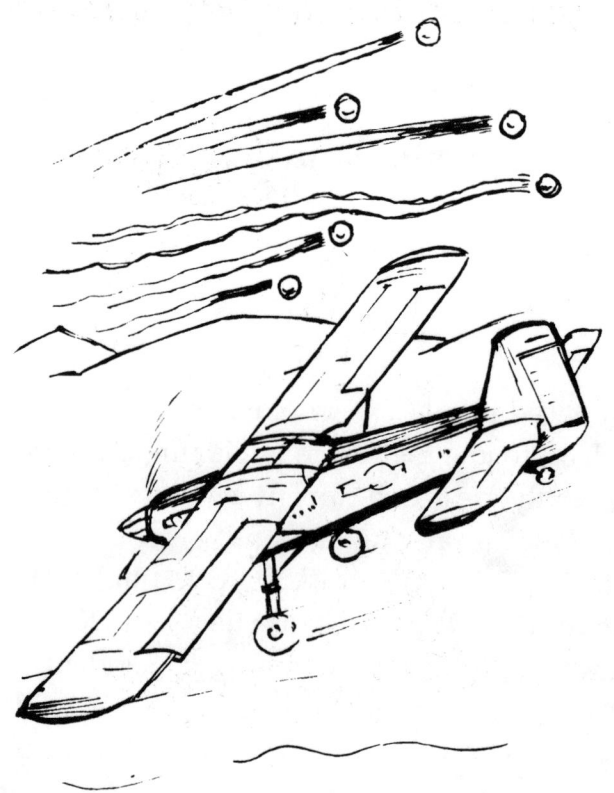

EXTRACT FROM THE EAST OREGONIAN

**Pendleton, Oregon, June 25.
Nine bright, saucer-like objects flying at incredible speed at 10,000 feet altitude were reported here today by Kenneth Arnold, a pilot from Boise, Idaho who said he could not hazard a guess as to what they were.**

Later, Arnold described the aircraft as flying like, 'a saucer would if you skipped it across the water.'

Ken Arnold's flying saucer sighting received massive publicity and within a month there were more than 100 sightings.

It was the dawn of the modern UFO age.

Here are some more Daylight Disc sightings:

Brazil, January 16, 1958: The crew of the Brazilian navy survey ship, Almirante Saldanha, were preparing to return to Rio de Janeiro from a voyage to an island survey station. On board was Almiro Barauna, a specialist in underwater photography.

Just after midday, the crew spotted something in the sky. Barauna grabbed his camera, trained it on the UFO and waited until it was silhouetted against a cloud before snapping it.

The UFO disappeared behind a mountain peak, then reappeared a few seconds later flying in the opposite direction. Barauna got it in the frame again and continued to take photographs.

Barauna developed his film on board ship in the presence of the captain, Commander Bacellar. As there was no photographic paper on board, he developed them on rice paper.

Back in Rio, the photographs were examined by experts who declared them genuine.

Kentucky, January 7, 1948: Some said it was like an 'upside-down ice-cream cone', others that it was 'umbrella-shaped.' Whatever shape it was, there was something strange in the sky near Fort Knox in Kentucky. Shortly after the reported sightings, six US Air National Guard F-51s were asked to investigate and took off just before 2.45 p.m. A little later one plane landed as its fuel tank was almost empty. When the remaining five reached 4500 metres (15,000 feet), two more headed back to base, followed at 6600 metres (22,000 feet) by another, leaving the last remaining plane, piloted by Captain Thomas Mantell.

Mantell radioed that whatever he was chasing was metallic and huge and moving at about half his speed. Half an hour after he took off, Mantell's plane vanished. At 5.00 p.m. the wreckage was found on a farm. Mantell's watch had stopped at 3.18 p.m.

Many people think that the dead pilot had been chasing a top-secret balloon being tested by the US Navy. Others are not so sure. They firmly believe that Thomas Mantell's plane was shot out of the sky by the crew of an alien spacecraft.

Kiev, August 1961:

Soviet air force pilots are a serious band of men, not given to flights of fancy. But the young man flying over the Ukraine swore that his plane was buzzed by a UFO – not only buzzed, but the alien aircraft seemed to be playing games with him. It flew round the bewildered pilot's plane in ever-decreasing circles, then just when it looked as if it was about to smash into the fighter's wings, it stopped circling and flew alongside, but keeping the same distance away.

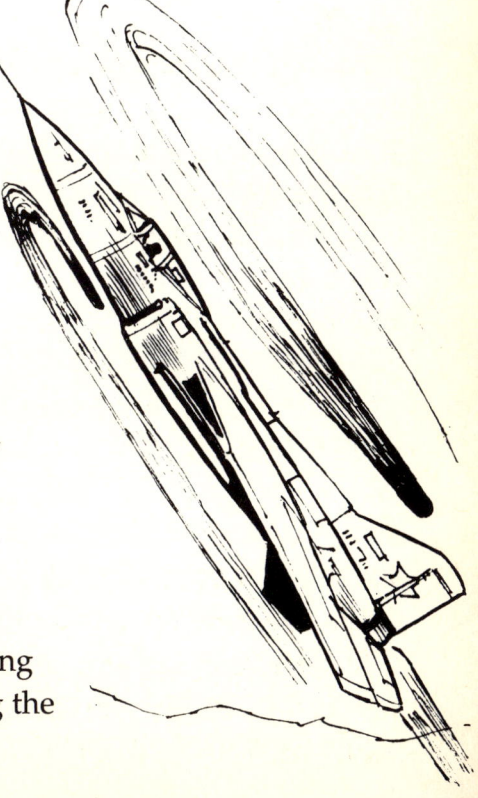

After twelve minutes the UFO backed off, accelerated to an incredible speed and vanished, leaving the astonished Russian to return to base as quickly as he could to tell his tale to the authorities.

Northern Honshu, October 17, 1975: It has to be said that some people who report UFO sightings are cranks – the kind of people you wouldn't believe if they told you it was midday when Big Ben was striking twelve o'clock. But Masaki Machida was a well-known and respected journalist working for a Japanese TV company. Waiting for a plane at Akita airport, Machida glanced upwards and saw a bright golden disc dotted with white lights coming in from the east.

When it was 8 kilometres (5 miles) from the airport and at an altitude of about 1500 metres (5000 feet), it stopped and hovered in the air.

Machida raced for a phone booth, called his news desk and reported the UFO sighting. This sighting was also witnessed by more than fifty others, including Captain Masaru Saito, pilot of a passenger aircraft flying nearby.

The investigation this sparked off turned up no unauthorized aircraft in the area, no top-secret plane being tested by the Japanese military, and no missing weather balloons.

To this day, the golden disc remains Unidentified.

Oregon, May 11, 1950: While Paul Trent's wife was feeding rabbits in the hutch in her yard just after 7.30 in the evening, she looked up and saw a bright silvery object floating towards the farm. Terrified, she called her husband, who didn't hear her. So, running into the house as fast as her feet would carry her, she grabbed a camera. She raced outside again and was in time to take two photographs of the UFO before it zoomed out of sight.

THE BLUE BOOK

There were so many UFOs seen in American skies immediately after Kenneth Arnold's sighting in Washington State in 1947 sparked off the modern UFO age, that in 1952, the United States Air Force decided to record and investigate each one. The project was known as 'The Blue Book.'

The first director was Captain Edward Ruppelt, and Dr J. Allen Hynek, one of the world's leading Ufologists, was later appointed its scientific adviser.

But many people believe that the US Air Force used The Blue Book whenever they could to disprove the existence of UFOs and to produce dubious evidence for a logical explanation for each reported sighting.

The Blue Book was closed in 1969, by which time Captain Ruppelt, who had gone into the Project with an open mind, had transferred to another job and written a book in which he stated not only his belief that UFOs did exist but also that the USAF were involved in a massive cover-up exercise.

Dr Hynek, having examined all the evidence, concluded there was a mystery that required proper investigation and went on to establish the Centre for UFO Studies.

Another expert, a scientist renowned for the scrupulousness of his research, not just into UFOs but in other fields as well, examined The Blue Book after the final chapter had been written. He described the USAF's investigations as 'completely super-ficial,' and carried out 'with a very low level of scientific competence.'

Most people who have snapshots of a UFO in their camera wouldn't wait until the film was finished before having it developed.

Most people with snapshots of a UFO in their photograph album would show them to as many people as possible.

The Trents were not like most people. When the film was eventually developed, they showed their photographs only to a handful of friends.

Experts disagreed when at last they saw the photographs. Some said they had been taken whole minutes, not just seconds, apart. Others claimed the so-called UFO was a mode[l] hanging from a string, or that the pictures were fakes and th[e] Trents were liars. But when, years later, the pictures wer[e]

THE BLUE BOOK

There were so many UFOs seen in American skies immediately after Kenneth Arnold's sighting in Washington State in 1947 sparked off the modern UFO age, that in 1952, the United States Air Force decided to record and investigate each one. The project was known as 'The Blue Book.'

The first director was Captain Edward Ruppelt, and Dr J. Allen Hynek, one of the world's leading Ufologists, was later appointed its scientific adviser.

But many people believe that the US Air Force used The Blue Book whenever they could to disprove the existence of UFOs and to produce dubious evidence for a logical explanation for each reported sighting.

The Blue Book was closed in 1969, by which time Captain Ruppelt, who had gone into the Project with an open mind, had transferred to another job and written a book in which he stated not only his belief that UFOs did exist but also that the USAF were involved in a massive cover-up exercise.

Dr Hynek, having examined all the evidence, concluded that there was a mystery that required proper investigation and went on to establish the Centre for UFO Studies.

Another expert, a scientist renowned for the scrupulousness of his research, not just into UFOs but in other fields as well, examined The Blue Book after the final chapter had been written. He described the USAF's investigations as 'completely super-ficial,' and carried out 'with a very low level of scientific competence.'

Most people who have snapshots of a UFO in their camera wouldn't wait until the film was finished before having it developed.

Most people with snapshots of a UFO in their photograph album would show them to as many people as possible.

The Trents were not like most people. When the film was eventually developed, they showed their photographs only to a handful of friends.

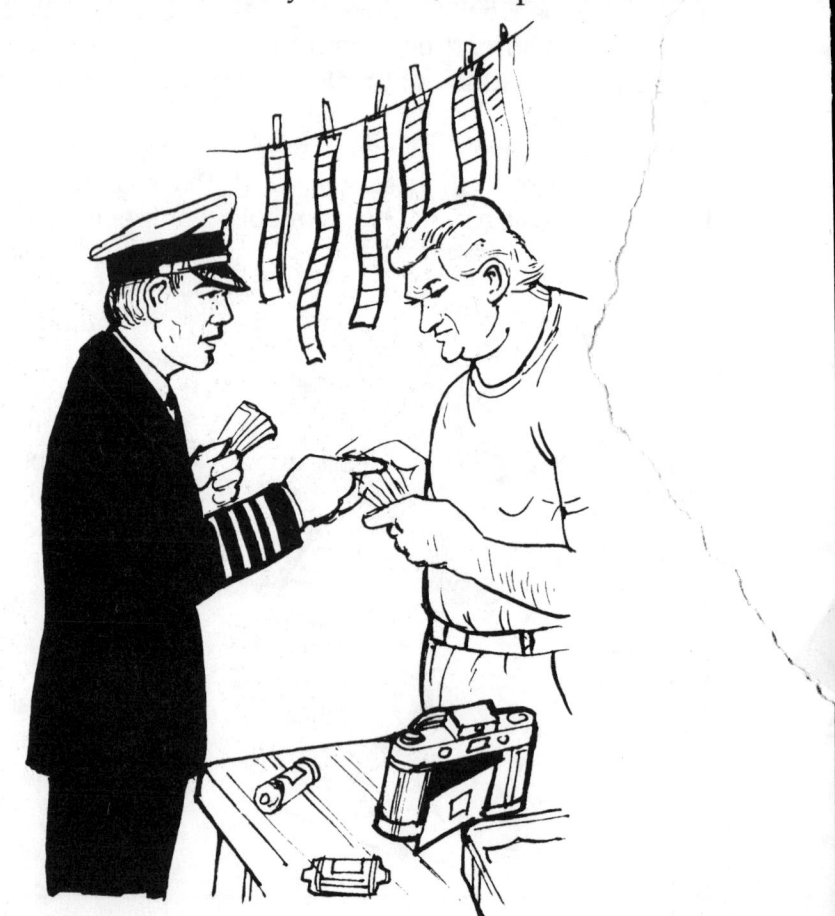

Experts disagreed when at last they saw the photographs. Some said they had been taken whole minutes, not just seconds, apart. Others claimed the so-called UFO was a model hanging from a string, or that the pictures were fakes and the Trents were liars. But when, years later, the pictures were digitally enhanced, there was no trace of any piece of string or wire and the expert who processed them estimated the Trent's UFO was 30 metres (100 feet) in diameter.

Was there something in the air that day or was it pie in the sky?

Washington DC, July 19, 1952: Just before midnight, radar screens picked up eight unknown objects flying in restricted air space over the White House. A few minutes later, airline pilots flying round the capital waiting for landing instructions reported a weird light in the sky flying at up to 480 km/h (300 mph), slowing to 160 km/h (100 mph) and then accelerating to mind-bending speeds.

Jets from New Jersey sped to the area, but by the time they got there, the UFOs had vanished.

As soon as the jets were back at base, the UFOs reappeared briefly, then vanished.

They were back a week later when as many as twelve were seen in the same area. Jets, this time from Delaware, were sent to investigate, but as soon as they appeared on the radar screen, the UFOs vanished and, just as before, the second the jets were out of Washington's radar scanners, the UFOs came back.

The US Air Force try to find logical explanations for every UFO sighting reported. But against the Washington entry in their lists are the words, 'Cause Unknown.'

Zimbabwe, July 22, 1985: So many people reported seeing something in the sky over six towns in Matabeleland that the Zimbabwean Air Force sent two Hawk interceptors to investigate.

They were the only things on the radar screens back at base, but the pilots reported that they had a round disc with a small cone on it in sight.

The radar operators looked again. Still there was nothing.

The planes flew in towards the UFO as it hovered in the air about 2000 metres (7000 feet) above the ground. Less than a minute later it had zoomed up to more than ten times that height.

To achieve that it must have broken the sound barrier, but there were no reports of a sonic boom.

The Hawks kept the UFO in sight until it disappeared from view.

And if Zimbabwean Air Force Marshall Azim Daudpota said in the official report, 'It was no illusion, no deception, no imagination,' who are we to disbelieve him?

EYEWITNESS

John Foster, now an electrician from Nebraska, USA, forgot all about what happened one night in the early 1950s for well over 30 years and then in 1986 when he was 49, disjointed memories of a holiday his family had had with his friend Bob and Bob's parents started to flood his mind. After a week or two of puzzling what they meant, he woke one night remembering more and all the pieces fitted together in a nightmarish jigsaw.

The two families were camping at Memphis State Lake in Nebraska and one afternoon when Bob and John were fishing, a curious disc-shaped object appeared out of a blue haze and hovered in the air above their heads.

They dropped their rods and tore back to the tents to get their parents.

Before John's father could stop them, Bob's family ran to their car and headed off in pursuit of whatever the two boys had seen. Mr and Mrs Foster decided to stay where they were with John and his two sisters but when two or three more objects appeared in the sky, looking as if they were moving in an electric force-field of some kind, John's father bundled the family into their car and headed for the other side of the lake.

As they turned a bend in the track, Mr Foster jammed on the brakes and the car screeched to a halt just before it looked certain it was about to slam into a solid-looking saucer-shaped object blocking their path.

They didn't hang around to find out what it was. John's father did a spectacular three-point turn and the car roared off down the track. But just before they got back to the campsite, the Fosters found another craft blocking their path.

As John stared at it, a voice filled his head, telling him to get out the car and walk toward the parked UFO. 'I remember opening the car door and following the instructions swimming about in my head, in a trance ignoring my parents' frantic calls,' said John all these years later. 'My dad must have got out the car and brought me down with a terrific [American] football tackle, for next thing I knew I was lying in the track, winded, Dad on top of me, his arms wrapped round my shoulders.'

As he lay there, he heard another car approach and a few moments later, Bob and his family were standing over him.

No sooner had he been helped to his feet than John saw the disk that had scared the pants off Bob and him earlier was now hovering near the other side of the lake. Before Mr Foster could stop him, Bob's father started to run round the lake towards it, but when he was quite close to it, there was a loud explosion and it backed off, before vanishing from sight.

Next thing John knew, what he says he can only describe as a booth with a door and windows appeared, hovering just above the the middle of the lake. Inside it, Bob's father could clearly be seen. Then a pillar of blue light shone from nowhere hitting the water just in front of where he was standing.

John's father plunged into the lake, and started to swim towards the booth but when he swam through the light he disappeared.

Terrified, Mrs Foster pushed her children into the car, got into the driver's seat and sped off round the lake.

John could still see Bob's father in the booth and although there was no sign of his own father, he could hear his voice yelling, 'What do you want? Just tell us what you want.'

'I don't know how long we stayed in the car,' said John. 'But eventually Mom drove back to the campsite where we were dumbfounded to find Dad and Bob's father waiting for us.

We kids were sent to bed right away and told to forget everything we had seen and heard.'

All the adults have long since died and when John questioned Bob about it more than 30 years later, his old friend claimed to have no memory of the event. And when John asked his sisters, quite separately, they both shuddered and a look of pure terror crossed their faces before they, too, shook their heads and said, 'I don't know what you're talking about.'

They have refused even to discuss for a moment with Bob what he knew happened at Memphis State Lake the day he saw the UFOs.

SPOOK FILES ENCYCLOPAEDIA

NOCTURNAL LIGHTS

There are literally hundreds of sightings of these mysterious lights that have never been properly accounted for, although many were undoubtedly the result of night-time test flights from top-secret air bases where new planes and missiles were being developed. Here are six of the best that have never been satisfactorily explained.

Bordeaux, November 14, 1971: It was well after midnight, but farmer Angelo Cellot was still hard at work trying to get the ploughing finished. Just before two o'clock he thought he saw the lights of another tractor coming towards him.

Then he realized the light was in the air and thought it was a helicopter. But why would a helicopter pilot beam five blinding spotlights on to a ploughman?

Would a helicopter hover threateningly overhead? Cellot didn't wait to find out. Abandoning his tractor, he ran for it.

As he raced across the field he realized that he had left the engine running. It was the only sound to be heard. Wouldn't a helicopter hovering overhead have made a deafening noise?

New Hampshire, September 3, 1965: It was 1.30 a.m when two policemen, Eugene Bertrand and David Hunt, spotted a badly parked car. On investigating, they found the female driver slumped over the wheel, too distressed at first to answer their questions.

When she recovered, she told the patrolmen that she had been followed by a UFO which, after tailing her for 20 kilometres (12 miles) had sped off at a speed that took her breath away.

Bertrand and Hunt calmed the woman down, saw her safely on her way and went back to the station. There they were dumbfounded to discover eighteen-year-old Norman Muscarello reporting a similar incident on the same road.

Bertrand volunteered to return to the spot with the teenager. 'We were astounded to see five red lights rise from behind a clump of trees. They were extremely bright,' Bertrand said later, 'and flashed on one at a time. The lights started to move around over a field and at one time came so close to me that I fell to the ground and drew my gun. There was no sound [apart from the panicked bleating of some nearby sheep], no vibrations.'

Bertrand and Muscarello both hot-footed it to the car where the officer radioed his partner Hunt, who arrived at the scene at around 3.00 a.m.

The lights were still flashing when Hunt got to the scene.

The three men watched them until at last they vanished. But by the time they got back to the station, a caller was on the line reporting from a phone box that a UFO was flying towards him.

The official explanation was that the UFO and lights were due to a USAF exercise that had been taking place in the area.

'What time did it finish?' Bertrand and Hunt asked.

'Two o'clock,' came the reply.

'We were still watching them at around three o'clock!'

The USAF then classified the sighting as, 'unknown'.

New Mexico, August 20, 1949: Clyde Tombaugh was no beginner when it came to skywatching. After all, in 1939, he had discovered the existence of the planet Pluto. Ten years later, as he scanned the night sky, he saw half a dozen or so rectangular lights flying in formation from the north-west to the south-east.

His wife and his mother-in-law saw them too.

Clyde, who worked at America's top-secret White Sands Missile Range a few miles away, was petrified, not just because he thought the Earth was about to be attacked, but also because he knew that if he reported what he had seen, many would scoff at him and his international reputation might be tarnished.

Consequently, he didn't report what he had seen right away.

When he did report it, one expert suggested that what he had seen were the lights of nearby towns reflected on a layer of ice-cold cloud.

Tombaugh disagreed, and until the day he died he believed he had seen something from another world.

New Mexico, August 25, 1951: It was nine o'clock at night when a security guard looked up and saw eight blue lights passing overhead in a V-shaped formation.

Twenty minutes later, four professors from a nearby college at Lubbock saw more lights, this time flying in semicircular formation.

Shortly after that, the area's USAF radar base picked up something on the screen, although there were no civilian or military flights scheduled to be in the area at that time.

A keen birdwatcher who lived near Lubbock said that what had been seen was a flight of plovers, the city lights reflected on their white breasts.

But is it likely that plovers could fly at 650 km/h (400 mph)?

Texas, November 2, 1957: Police at the small town of Levelland shook their heads in disbelief when local farmworker Pedro Saucedo told them he had been driving his truck home when a 60 metre (200 foot) yellow, torpedo-shaped light came out of the sky and drifted towards him.

The closer it got, the dimmer his headlights became, and when it was only a few feet away they went out altogether and the engine died. Pedro jumped out as the light passed overhead and felt a blast of heat.

As the yellow light moved away, the truck's lights came on again, and when Pedro pressed the ignition button, the engine immediately roared into life.

The sceptical police made notes as they were duty bound to do, thinking that that was the end of the matter.

Next day the town was buzzing with what Pedro had seen – and with the tale of a man called Jim Wheeler, whose car headlights had also faded and his engine died when a red light floated over his car a few miles east of town – and of the local sheriff who swerved off the road to avoid a red light blocking the road ahead!

Vietnam, June 1966: Throughout the 1960s American troops were on active service in Vietnam and the sky was full of USAF planes taking off and returning from bombing sorties.

But no plane was responsible for the brilliant light that appeared in the sky north of the US base at Nha Tranh.

Why did the light move closer to the base? Why did it then stop and hover above the base? Why was there a total power failure at the base?

Why did all the lights go out on a tanker anchored in a nearby bay and why did her engines stop?

And why was power restored three or four minutes after the bright light vanished?

The scores of hard-bitten US marines who witnessed the incident have no explanation either.

SPOOK FILES ENCYCLOPAEDIA

RADAR VISUALS

Electronic interference causing blips in the bleeps – or Aliens keeping an eye on us? Make up your mind from the following cases where UFOs have not only been seen but have been picked up by experienced radar operators on their screens. Here's a quartet of radio-visual sightings of inquisitive UFOs.

Iran, September 19, 1976: So many people in Iran reported something in the sky just after midnight that the Iranian Air Force scrambled two F-4 Phantoms from the Shahroki air base, 200 kilometres (125 miles) away from the sighting. The first closed in on the UFO, but when it was still 40 kilometres (25 miles) away, the plane's communication system died and the pilot backed off. The radar on the second jet suggested that the object people had seen was about the size of a short-haul passenger jet. When the pilot took his plane to within 40 kilometres (25 miles) of the UFO, which was now flashing rectangular-patterned strobe lights (the kind that dazzle you in a disco), it moved away and kept a constant distance between itself and the Iranian jet.

Suddenly the pilot saw something leave the UFO and shoot through the sky towards him. He tried to fire a missile at it, but the light on his weapon-control panel dimmed and, as it faded away, his radio went dead.

Whatever was streaking towards the Phantom then U-turned and sped back to the UFO. Not surprisingly, the pilot headed for home and, as he came in to land, the UFO flashed overhead and was seen by several of the ground staff.

An Iranian illusion or a close encounter of the Phantom kind?

New Zealand, December 31, 1978: Just before Christmas, the radar on an Argosy cargo plane flying south-west from Blenheim on New Zealand's South Island, picked up a UFO and moments later the crew's eyes widened as something appeared in the sky ahead.

When the story hit the papers, an Australian TV crew flew to New Zealand, and ten days after the sighting was reported, took off from Wellington, flew across the Cook Strait heading for Blenheim to pick up the same flight path as the Argosy.

Twenty-five minutes after takeoff the crew reported lights ahead and something was picked up on Wellington radar. Ten minutes later there was another sighting and the camera crew started filming.

Just after 1.00 a.m. the plane landed at Christchurch, refuelled and headed back for Wellington. As it broke through a bank of clouds, a dazzling UFO appeared straight ahead, and far below radar screens picked up a huge object flying some 30 kilometres (19 miles) from the plane.

Again the cameras started to whirr, and when the film was processed, an oval body with rings of light around it could be clearly seen.

A planet, said some.

A phenomenon caused by a layer of warm air coming into contact with a layer of hot air, said others.

Lights from fishing boats reflected in the clouds was another suggestion.

If any of these theories was right, why did the New Zealand Air Force keep a jet on permanent standby for several weeks afterwards to intercept any more UFOs that might appear in the Southern skies?

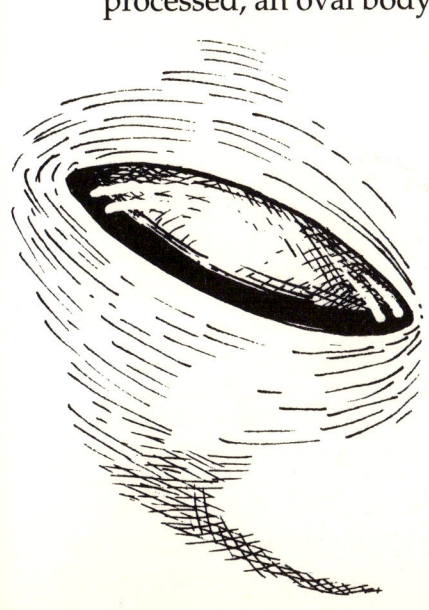

Russia, Summer 1961: There was definitely something in the air near Moscow that summer day as workers laboured on installing a missile defence system around the city. In fact, there were several things in the air – for Russian radar picked up a massive object surrounded by smaller ones, flying at 18,000 metres (60,000 feet).

Never people to hang around and wait to be attacked, the Russians launched a salvo of missiles at the UFO fleet from the Rybinsk base 255 kilometres (160 miles) north of the capital. As the rockets streaked through the sky, the smaller UFOs lost altitude and it seemed to observers that they were making for the base.

Suddenly, the Russian electronic equipment went dead and the missiles blew up well short of their target.

The escort UFOs then returned to the mother ship and, as they bleeped off the radar screen, the lights and other equipment at the Rybinsk base came to life again.

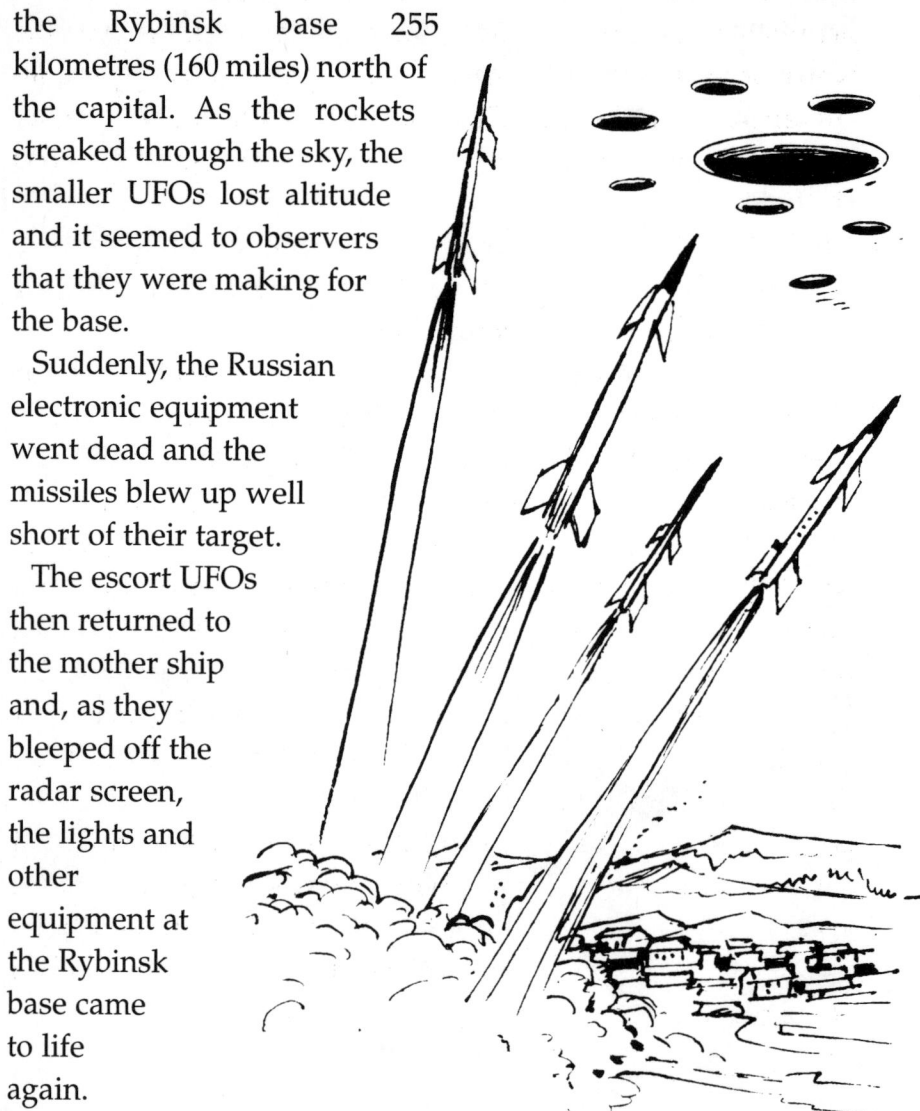

United Kingdom August 13, 1956: During the Cold War, the period when many thought that real war could erupt at any time between the USA and the USSR, any unscheduled aircraft flying east to west across Europe was regarded with dark suspicion by the West. This was especially true in the air space over England's East Anglia, where the US Air Force had several air bases.

Just before 11.00 p.m. on August 13, the radar screen at Bentwaters air base picked up something zooming over the North Sea at 6540 km/h (4000 mph), a speed faster by far than any aircraft could reach. The object flew over the base before vanishing from the radar screen about 50 kilometres (32 miles) to the west.

Two eyewitnesses – a control tower operator and a USAF pilot flying a C-4 – confirmed seeing something hurtling through the sky at an unbelievable speed.

Minutes after it vanished from the Bentwaters screen, it was picked up once more on radar at the nearby Lakenheath base. And it seemed to be barnstorming through the sky, treating those who saw it to a dazzling display of aerial acrobatics.

The RAF were alerted and sent up two Venom NF2a jet fighters. As soon as the first got one within range, the UFO flipped over like a tossed coin, positioned itself behind the plane, and nothing the pilot did could shake it from his tail.

As soon as the second Venom arrived on the scene, whatever was at the UFO's controls withdrew, and it was last seen on radar screens speeding north.

The official report on the sighting said that the UFO had behaved in a rational, intelligent way, and suggested that it was a mechanical device of unknown origin. Is that a bureaucratic way of saying a UFO came visiting with an alien at the controls?

SPOOK FILES ENCYCLOPAEDIA

STOP PRESS STOP PRESS PRESS STOP PRESS STOP

BOSTON EXCITED OVER PHANTOM AEROPLANE

Worcester, December 24, 1922:
Flying through the night at an average speed of 20 to 40 miles per hour, a mysterious airship appeared over Worcester shortly before six o'clock, hovered briefly over the city, disappeared and returned to cut four circles, meanwhile sweeping the heavens with a searchlight of tremendous power.

The glaring rays of the great searchlight were sharply defined by reflection against the light snowfall which covered the city. The dark mass of the airship could be dimly seen behind the light which flashed in all directions. An airship that no one admitted was in the area on that wintry night on America's east coast, one of many natural phenomena, or something more sinister?

EYEWITNESS

One cold winter night in December 1966, Walter Arden, a San Francisco businessman and chairman of a local German/American association, had just closed its usual monthly meeting and was writing up the minutes so he could turn off the lights and go home.

There was only one other member of the association there, Richard Decker, a frail seventy-year-old who ran a local engineering business, and who was putting on his overcoat. Walter always liked Richard, although he didn't have many friends in the association, probably, Walter thought, because he was so reserved. He rarely came to any of the social events the association organized and Walter hardly ever saw him laugh or smile.

When Richard spoke, he always came straight to the point and this had earned him the reputation among other members for saying nothing other than the truth. 'You can always trust what Richard says,' several members had remarked. And it was because of this that Walter held Richard in some esteem and liked to think of him as a friend.

He had just about finished the minutes when Richard came over to shake hands and say good night. Walter looked up and noticed a small, silvery ornament in the lapel of Richard's overcoat. It looked like a small, shiny flower.

'What's that?' he asked, reaching out to touch it.

'Walter, I always wear this . . .' Richard said falteringly and then paused before going on to tell him that he always made a point of leaving the club last in case any of the others noticed the lapel pin.

Walter was flattered when Richard told him that he liked and trusted him and didn't mind that he had spotted it. Then he said, 'If I tell you what it is, you must promise never to divulge what I'm about to say.'

Walter nodded in agreement.

Richard ran a finger over his pin and said, 'This is how we recognize each other.'

'Recognize who?' Walter asked.

'Walter,' smiled Richard. 'I am not of this world. I come from a planet you will never have heard of. There are thousands of us here on Earth.'

'Come off it, Richard,' said Walter, expecting the older man to punch him playfully and tell him he had been joking. But no punch came. No, 'I'm having you on of course, but I had you going though.'

'Richard,' gulped Walter. 'I happen to know you were born in Germany and that you came to the States to study engineering. It's in the club records. You've been a member here longer than anyone else.'

Richard nodded and told Walter that what he had said was true; he had indeed been born in Germany and had come to the States to study, but he went on to say that when one of his race was sent on a secret mission, they were given the power to take over the body of an unborn baby in the mother's womb and come into the world as if they were newborn human.

'Our earth families are usually chosen because they are wealthy, or at least affluent, so they will send us to good schools and pay for us to study a profession – medicine, the law, engineering, something like that,' Richard said.

Walter shook his head in disbelief when Richard went on to tell him that he and the others of his race could even get married and have children.

'But by then we will have started on whatever mission we have been sent here to accomplish.'

'Mission?' Walter gasped, 'What is your mission?'

'I can't tell you that,' Richard replied. 'All I can say is that when we reach old age – human old age that is – we are called home. I'll be going quite soon. I just wanted to tell you how much I have appreciated your friendship over the years. I'll be back again, though. This is my fourth mission, but I don't expect I'll be sent on a new one in your lifetime.'

After reminding him that he had promised to keep his secret, Richard shook Walter's hand and left the room.

Walter was so stunned that he had to sit for quite a while to collect his thoughts. What he had just been told couldn't possibly be true. But there was something so compelling in the way Richard had talked that made him think that perhaps it was.

Richard continued to come to meetings, was always last to leave and never again mentioned the conversation, and Walter, true to his word, kept his silence.

Then, fifteen months later, Richard disappeared, vanished without a trace and has never been seen or heard of again.

Walter kept his secret for 28 years before he told his family. 'After that length of time,' he wrote, 'Richard would have considered my promise fulfilled.'

SPOOK FILES ENCYCLOPAEDIA

THE ALIENS ARE HERE

Aliens come in all shapes and sizes, but before we move on to Close Encounters of the First and later kinds, let's look at the most common types of aliens that have been seen.

The Apparition

It was just before midnight on March 17, 1978, when the driver of a car taking a short cut down a quiet road close to the UK Atomic Energy Centre at Risley in Cheshire had to slam on the brakes and come to a skidding halt. Something had suddenly appeared in the road ahead. It was white, had two arms, and two large eyes in an otherwise featureless face.

Frozen to the spot, the driver watched in horror as beams of light shot from those eyes and focused on his hands which were gripped tight round the steering wheel.

The figure moved on, then walked straight through the 3 metre (10 feet) high security fence around the atomic plant.

The bewildered man looked at his watch. It had stopped at 11.45 p.m. He unhooked his CB radio to report what had happened. It was defunct.

He felt a tingling in his hands, and when he held them up, he discovered they were covered in blisters where the light beams had hit them.

Aliens such as this are called Apparitions. One expert has recorded over 120 apparition sightings.

The Dwarf

If you ever come across a small, dark green, hairy creature with large ears, look out, for an alien of this type is aggressive and may attack. Dwarves were seen in South America several times during the 1950s, and have been witnessed in France.

A French steel worker had the following extraordinary experience in 1954. He was walking with his dog late at night near Valenciennes, close to the Belgian border.

Letting the dog off the leash to have a good run, he was astonished when, a few moments later, the poor creature came racing back to him, whimpering in fear.

Shining his torch in the direction the dog had come from, he saw what had terrorized his dog – two dwarf aliens. As soon as he spotted them, he was caught in a beam of brilliant light and found himself totally paralysed.

He stood there, rooted to the spot, until the light went out and the two aliens floated skywards to a waiting UFO, which then shot off in a blaze of red light.

The police scoffed at his story – but later several people came forward to report seeing a strange, red light flashing through the sky that night.

The Goblin

Hundreds of people claim to have seen troll-like aliens that look as if they have stepped straight from the pages of a Scandinavian storybook. One of these was caught on camera at Ilkley in Yorkshire in December 1987.

It was about half-past seven in the morning when an ex-police officer was tramping across Ilkley Moor to visit his father-in-law. A sudden movement on his right caught his eye, and when he looked he was astonished to see a little green creature close by. It was about 1.3 metres (3 feet) tall. It had spindly arms and legs, sausage-like fingers, a slit mouth, large dark eyes and long ears.

The man reached for the camera he happened to be carrying but by the time he had taken it out of its case, the alien began to run away. While it was still in sight, it turned, and as it waved its right arm in what was later described as 'a dismissive gesture,' the alien was caught on film.

The man chased after it as far as a bluff, but when he rounded it the creature had vanished and a silvery UFO was hovering overhead.

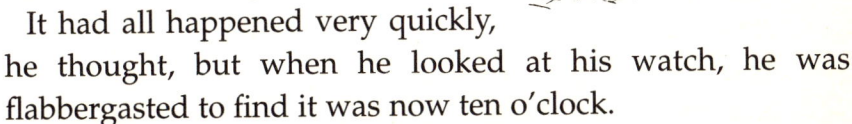

It had all happened very quickly, he thought, but when he looked at his watch, he was flabbergasted to find it was now ten o'clock.

Goblin aliens often appear in places long associated with devil worship and some people believe that goblins are not aliens at all, but evil spirits returning to haunt particular spots. But goblins like the one on Ilkley Moor have been seen near UFOs, which suggests they may indeed come from outer space.

The Greys

Well over half of the aliens seen over the past ten years are known as the greys – small, usually less than 1.3 metres (4.5 feet) tall, with large, round, insect-like eyes that dominate their faces. They send shivers down the spines of all those who have met them.

Greys get their name from their spooky colour and are the villains responsible for many a human abduction. It is said that greys often perform experiments on those unfortunate enough to be taken on board one of their spacecraft.

Their experiments are not always malicious, according to one Chicago woman with chronic sinusitis who was taken aboard a UFO by a troop of greys. When she told them of her malady she was set down gently into a state-of-the-art dentist's chair. One of them spoke to her in a soothing voice, then carefully pushed a small wand up her nose. In an instant her sinusitis had gone!

The Nordics

With long blond hair and piercing blue eyes, the Nordics are the glamour boys of the alien world. They are tall, usually around 1.8 metres (6 feet), and have slanting eyes. About a quarter of alien encounters are with Nordics.

They are usually friendly and often warn those who see and talk to them that the Earth is in danger on two fronts, first from the greys and second from nuclear energy, which they say may be fatal to the Earth's ecology.

It was a Nordic that visited Maria Pretzel in June 1968 at the motel her father owned in Villa Carlos, a small Argentinian town 800 km (500 miles) west of Buenos Aires.

As she was going to bed, she noticed a light on in the hall. When she went to turn it off, she came face to face with a tall, fair-haired alien. The alien smiled and spoke to her. Although he used a language she couldn't understand, she was sure he was trying to say something good and kind to her.

After a minute or two, he let himself out. It was about ten to one. A little later her father, who had been out, arrived home to find the motel bathed in brilliant red light, which faded immediately he got out of his car.

The Robot

Rarely appearing on their own, robots are usually seen with other alien species, who use them as their assistants. A Russian boy had experience of this one day when he fell and hurt his knee while playing at his home near Tbilisi.

As he lay on the ground unable to move, some greys and robots appeared. The robots held the boy down as one of the greys manipulated the boy's knee, and moments later, he was as right as rain.

Robotic aliens have smooth and shiny bodies, move clumsily, and range in size from mini to massive. Some robots are as quiet as mice, others have been heard to roar like lions.

SPOOK FILES ENCYCLOPAEDIA

CLOSE ENCOUNTERS OF THE FIRST KIND

Australia-New Zealand, 1931: It had been only thirty years since the Wright Brothers had made their historic first flight in a mechanically powered aircraft, but already brave airmen were flying into the record books and Francis Chichester was determined to join them. The thirty-year-old Englishman was at the controls of a Gypsy Moth plane on course to make the first flight across the Tasman Sea from Australia to his home in New Zealand. He was already well into his flight when flashing lights moving at high speed above him captured his attention.

He watched, terrified, as a large object shaped like a silvery pearl closed in, hovered round the plane as if it was investigating it, then shot off again.

Many years later, in 1996-7, Chichester was to sail single-handed round the world, a voyage that brought many close encounters with danger, but none as petrifying as his close encounter in the skies above the Tasman Sea.

England, October 1967: Angus Brooks, a retired RAF Intelligence officer, was in no doubt about seeing an object in the sky that was not of this world.

Two days before, while Brooks was taking his two dogs for a walk on the windswept downs on the south coast of Dorset, two police patrolmen from neighbouring Devon had followed what they described as a vast illuminated cross for 20 kilometres (12 miles) as it skirted the fringes of Dartmoor. Many other people in the area also reported seeing a strange object in the sky.

Brooks was unaware of this as he strode across the downs. Suddenly the wind rose and he was forced to take shelter behind a bluff.

Looking up to watch the clouds scudding across the sky, he saw a vapour trail in the south-west. As he watched, he realized it was coming from an aircraft resembling nothing he had ever seen before.

Losing speed quickly, it came to a stop about 75 metres (250 feet) above the ground and about 350 metres (400 yards) from where he was sheltering. Protruding from a central disc 8 metres (25 feet) in diameter and 3.5 metres (12 feet) thick was a 'girder-like' fuselage jutting forward with three others behind it, all about 22 metres (75 feet) long.

Brooks watched in amazement as the two outer tails at the rear swung round until they were at an angle of 90 degrees to the other two, so forming a cross with the disc in the middle.

There was enough time for him to see that the craft had no windows and seemed to be made of a shiny material that changed colour, as if it was camouflaging itself to blend in with the constantly changing sky.

Twenty-two minutes later, the UFO reverted to its original shape and flew off.

The authorities said that Brooks must have fallen asleep as he sheltered from the wind.

Could you sleep with a force eight gale howling and two dogs pawing at you in terror?

SPOOK FILES ENCYCLOPAEDIA

Gloucestershire, England, March 1988: Edwin Rochester (not his real name: many people who see UFOs ask not to be identified for fear of being ridiculed) was washing up after dinner, when he looked out of the window and saw a light moving across a nearby field.

At first he thought it was a local shepherd checking for foxes, but then he realized that the light was too far above the ground to be carried by a human. He stepped cautiously out into his garden to investigate. But when he reached his fence, the light disappeared.

He was about to go back into the house when suddenly he was bathed in light and, looking up, he saw a great shining ball swirling round in the air above his head.

To add to his amazement, he realized that he alone was caught in the ball's beam, not even the ground he was standing on was lit up.

What happened next is difficult to believe, but Edwin later swore it was true. A voice spoke to him.

It told him that he was looking at a probe sent with a warning from another galaxy. Its inhabitants were concerned that technology on Earth was advancing at an alarming rate, and they feared it might get out of control and cause untold damage to the universe.

'What will you do if that should happen?' Edwin asked. The reply was chilling. The aliens, said the voice, would introduce bacteria and viruses for which Earth had no antidotes.

And with that, the light faded, leaving a dumbfounded Gloucestershire man in the dark.

England, April 1991: Flying at a height of 6,750 metres (22,000 feet), the captain of an Alitalia McDonnell Douglas MD-80 was on his descent into a London airport when he and his co-pilot saw a 3 metre (10 foot) long brown missile above them, heading south-east.

He immediately radioed air traffic control, who confirmed that they had something on radar close to the plane, and that it was travelling at nearly 800 km/h (500 mph).

No sooner had the message come through than the UFO vanished into thin air.

Himalayas, August 1929: It was half-past nine in the morning when Nicholas Roerich and other members of an expedition trekking in the Himalayas were getting ready to leave their camp on the next leg of their journey.

'Look,' someone shouted, pointing upwards at a black eagle soaring above them. For a time the men were enthralled at the sight of the majestic bird in flight. Suddenly there was a yell. 'Look, there's something very odd flying above the bird.'

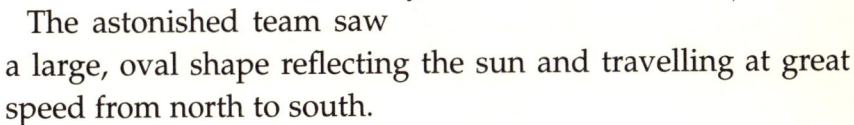

The astonished team saw a large, oval shape reflecting the sun and travelling at great speed from north to south.

It remained in view long enough for the men to track it through their binoculars, and all of them noted its oval shape and glittering surface.

Of course, everyone scoffed at their tale when they got back to Europe, but Roerich and the others remained convinced until the day they died that they had had an uncomfortably close encounter with something from outer space.

Sweden, Summer 1933: Not once, but twelve times in the long summer days of 1933, a UFO was seen by the parish priest at Lantrask, a small town in northern Sweden. On one occasion it flew so low that he could see two shadowy figures in the cabin. At first he thought it was a plane flying off course, but when it came close enough for him to see the markings which all planes must carry, there were none. No amateur pilot ever confessed to flying over the area and there were no military flights reported.

Nor was the pastor the first to report seeing a flying object over Scandinavia. Between 1932 and 1937 there were hundreds of sightings, often in weather conditions when conventional aircraft would have been grounded.

Witnesses talked of single-winged flying machines with as many as eight engines. They spoke of their engines being cut, even in foul weather conditions, and of aircraft circling overhead like great condors about to sweep down in search of carrion.

Some observers found themselves bathed in powerful lights, and others saw coloured lights flying overhead, making definite patterns in the sky.

Throughout Scandinavia there were rumours that a secret airbase lay somewhere in the Arctic Circle, for these flying objects travelled south over northern Norway and Sweden before turning north and flying over Finland.

Planes from the Swedish Air Force took to the Arctic skies to look for this base, but found nothing. Nor did the crews of planes sent in from Norway.

Were they UFOs that haunted the Scandinavian skies in the 1930s? To this day, no one knows for sure.

New Guinea, 1959: Father William Mechoir Gill, a missionary working in Papua New Guinea, finished dinner early one evening in June and was taking a stroll round the missionary compound before darkness fell.

Overhead, the planet Venus was already shining brightly, but as Father William gazed upwards, first one, then another strange object appeared in the sky. More dazzling than Venus, they were cigar-shaped and about 620 metres (2000 feet) high. They rose and fell lazily like boats in a gentle swell.

Suddenly a wind blew in clouds from the west and, as they scudded by, each cloud was ringed by a halo of light reflected by the flying objects.

Fascinated, Father William watched the display of lights, then fascination turned to disbelief as human-like figures emerged from one of the spaceships and began to move to and fro, like a busy crew on the deck of a ship.

Father William was not the sole witness of this extraordinary spectacle. Others at the mission – teachers, nurses, medical students and children – had gathered to gaze up in wonderment. For more than an hour, they watched before the alien spaceships vanished.

Returning to his quarters, Father William made careful notes of all he had seen and next morning had them read and signed by twenty-five fellow witnesses.

The next evening, Father William was working in his study when a Papuan girl burst in to tell him breathlessly that the spaceships had returned.

The sun was setting but there was more than enough light for the priest to see four aliens moving about on the deck of what seemed to be the 'mother' ship, while two smaller ships hovered nearby.

Father William's notes read, 'Two of the figures seemed to be doing something. They were occasionally bending over and raising their arms as though adjusting or setting something up.'

When one of the aliens seemed to be looking down, Father William waved both arms, and to his amazement, the alien waved back. Then all four aliens on deck began waving to the watchers below.

When darkness began to fall, one of the missionary boys ran to collect a torch and when he returned began to flash Morse Code dots and dashes up to the aliens. The creatures responded by making pendulum-like motions with their arms.

The watchers made more signals, trying to suggest that the spacecraft should land, and at first it seemed as if it might. But then the aliens disappeared into their ship and after lingering for thirty or so minutes longer, all three UFOs shot out of sight.

A little later there was the sound of a tremendous explosion and everyone at the mission station again raced outside, but there was nothing to be seen.

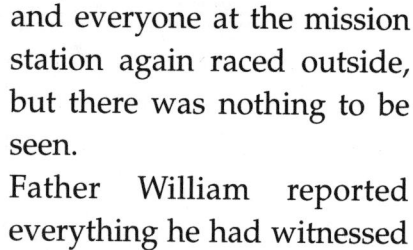

Father William reported everything he had witnessed to the Australian Air Attaché at Port Moresby, capital of Papua New Guinea, who in turn reported it to the US Air Force.

Neither the Australians nor the Americans could offer an explanation. The suggestion was that the stars or planets had been responsible for the seemingly unearthly phenomenon, but as leading ufologist J. Allen Hynek pointed out, 'I have yet to observe stars or planets appearing to descend through the clouds to a height of 620 metres (2000 feet), illuminating the clouds as they did so.'

Father William and all the other observers at his mission had no doubts. They had definitely seen UFOs 'manned' by alien beings.

Wales, 1976: Mrs Marion Sunderland was alarmed when her nine-year-old daughter, Gaynor, ran home one summer's day, scared out of her wits. She calmed and comforted the child and listened with growing amazement to the tale she had to tell.

Gaynor had been walking in the fields close to the family house in Oakenholt, Flint, when suddenly she felt cold. Looking up to see if the sun had gone in, she saw a silver saucer-shaped spacecraft hanging in the air.

Shivering, not with cold but with terror, she ran behind a hedge and threw herself on to the ground.

Peering through a gap in the hedge she saw the spacecraft land in a field.

The flying saucer was about 12 metres (39 feet) long and less than 3 metres (10 feet) high. She gazed at it, her heart thumping against her chest, and when, after a few minutes nothing happened, she decided to make a dash for home. But just as she stood up, a door slid open and two silver-suited aliens got out.

Gaynor threw herself down again and watched as the short, awkward, pink-eyed creatures began to probe the ground with what looked like metal-detecting machines.

Only a few minutes passed before they returned to the spaceship, but to Gaynor it seemed like hours.

With a loud humming noise and a flash of light, the spacecraft rose up, hovered briefly just above the ground, and then shot off into the sky.

Petrified, Gaynor lay where she was for several minutes more, then got to her feet and ran back to the house as fast as she could.

Mrs Sunderland had no doubt that her daughter was telling the truth, and she wanted to call the police immediately, but Gaynor begged her not to as she was sure they would just laugh at her.

For the next 18 months the Sunderlands said nothing, but eventually couldn't keep the story to themselves any longer.

It came to the attention of Jenny Randles, one of Britain's great UFO experts. She visited the Sunderlands and felt certain that Gaynor had not made up the story. But just to make sure, she suggested hypnotism.

Gaynor was hypnotized not once, but twice. And both times she told the same story, right down to the very last detail.

Gaynor's description of the spacecraft and the aliens is one of the most detailed ever recorded.

Northern England, 1976, 1978 and 1979: Fencehouses in Tyne and Wear and the towns and villages around it are the sort of places where nothing extraordinary every happens. At least, until 1976 nothing extraordinary ever happened. But in

September of that year, two women who even now ask that their names should be withheld, were enjoying a walk near their homes in Fencehouses when a small silvery object landed just in front of them.

They wanted to turn and run away, but they couldn't. They were rooted to the spot, then as if being pulled by a magnet, they found themselves drawn towards it.

Two doll-like creatures alighted. Pure white hair tumbled around their faces from which shone two piercing eyes.

At the sight of the two women the aliens looked startled and retreated hurriedly to their spaceship, whereupon it immediately dissolved right before the eyes of two shocked and mystified women.

Seventeen months later, at nearby Killingworth, a young nurse saw a UFO flying between two houses. The noise it made was so deafening that her mother hid under her bedclothes, convinced a plane was about to crash.

It was no plane. Looking out of the window, the young woman saw a silvery object decked with bright light hovering in the air for a moment, before zooming back through the gap in the houses opposite.

Three years after that first sighting at Fencehouses, another young woman living in the same area woke early to a gloomy pre-sunrise light, and saw a bell-like disc floating towards her through her bedroom window.

As it hovered above her head, a soft buzzing filled the air and the petrified woman felt as if her muscles had been turned to stone. She could neither move nor call for help.

As in 1976, doll-like creatures appeared from the disc, but when they saw the woman, they scuttled back and the disc floated out through the window a few seconds later.

As we said, Fencehouses and the towns around are the sort of places where nothing much happens – unless you count the weird visitations of 1976, 1978 and 1979.

France, 1965: Lavender farmer Marcel Masse thought he had spotted two boys stealing lavender plants from his fields in southern France, and was about to reprimand them when they turned round and stopped him dead in his tracks. They weren't boys, but creatures with large heads, enormous staring eyes and long, jutting chins.

Marcel recovered enough to move towards the aliens, but no sooner had he taken the first step than one of them pointed a stick at him and he couldn't move a muscle.

They eyed him suspiciously for a second or two before floating upwards in a beam of light. Freed from their spell, Marcel looked up to see a spacecraft floating overhead. Six legs appeared to hang from its circular centre.

He watched as it started to throb with light before flipping over and vanishing into space. He ran forward and found himself standing in the middle of a bone-dry patch of earth below the spot where the spaceship had hovered.

When he returned to examine the dry patch the next day, the lavender around it had withered and died, and for years after no lavender would take root there and grow.

Voronezh, Russia, 1989: Voronezh is a sleepy town 480 kilometres (300 miles) south of Moscow. But it woke up one October night when several witnesses saw a spherical object land in the local park. Shortly after the landing two aliens with enormous bodies and tiny heads were seen.

They were not alone. With them was a small, robot-like creature.

The aliens did not linger. A few minutes later they strode back to their UFO, which took off as soon as they were aboard.

People who had seen them couldn't sleep for weeks afterwards, and when they did manage to drop off from sheer weariness, they woke again in the middle of the night, sweating profusely.

During the day they were seized by panic attacks during which their hearts beat madly and they had to fight for every breath they took.

It wasn't long before the authorities in Moscow heard about the incident and sent experts to investigate. When the frightened townspeople of Voronezh pointed out where the UFO had come down, the men from Moscow found marks that looked as if an aircraft had landed, and also four curious depressions in the ground.

There has never been an official explanation of what was seen at Voronezh, but curiously a dairymaid from a town 1120 kilometres (700 miles) away reported seeing giants with small heads emerge from a spacecraft that landed shortly after two orange flashes had lit up the night sky.

She had no connection whatsoever with anyone who lived in Voronezh and no one in that town had ever heard of her.

Florida, USA, 1987 and 1988: Estate agent and property developer Edward Walters hasn't had just one close encounter, but several. The first was in November 1987 when he glanced out of his office window and saw a UFO travelling slowly above the trees.

Ed Walters always kept a camera in his desk to photograph properties he was asked to sell. But it wasn't a house he focused on that day. After taking several photographs of the UFO from his office window, he dashed outside to take some more.

No sooner had he reached the street than he was trapped in a beam of blue light, quite unable to move. As he struggled in vain to free himself, his nostrils were filled with the scent of spices, and he felt himself being lifted up from the ground.

At the same time, a voice that seemed to be in his head whispered over and over again, 'We will not harm you. We will not harm you.'

He was still trying to move about when suddenly the light that held him vanished, and with it the UFO.

Edward saw the UFO again on two more occasions and each time the chain of events was almost the same.

Three weeks after the first sighting when the UFO arrived, an alien appeared in Edward's garden and the voice in his head whispered, 'Do not be afraid.'

Six weeks later, he was driving home along a quiet road when the UFO appeared again. Edward came to a skidding halt and, as on his first encounter, he began to photograph it. He was again bathed in a beam of bright blue light and again he was unable to move.

Ufologists have questioned Edward Walters over and over again and even the most cynical have been impressed by the fact that his story has never changed, no matter how many times he has told it.

Disbelievers scoffed and said Ed Walters made it all up, but experts have examined his photographs and believe them to be genuine.

So Ed Walters is a real estate agent who has had at least three real close encounters of the first kind.

Wales, 1978: Two boys were playing football just before nightfall on a patch of wasteland outside the small village of Llanerchymedd.

'Look!' cried one boy. 'That helicopter's about to land.'

But what they saw was no helicopter. Instead, a bullet-shaped object glowing red was coming in to land behind a clump of trees.

The boys ran to watch. Other people in the village had heard the noise and were running too.

Two 2 metre (6.3 feet) figures clad in grey suits emerged from the spacecraft and were walking towards the astounded onlookers. Horses grazing in a field nearby snorted and reared up in fright.

The villagers rushed off to tell the police, but by the time they arrived, the aliens and their spacecraft had vanished, leaving no trace. But for many days afterwards, the frightened horses were quite uncontrollable.

West Virginia, 1952: Thousands of people saw the glowing ball streak through the sky above the hills of West Virginia one night in mid-September. At the small town of Sutton, several people thought they saw it land, and five of them, Kathleen May, her three young sons and seventeen-year-old National Guardsman Gene Lemon, set off to investigate.

They climbed towards the spot and when they were close, Gene swept the area with his torch.

At precisely the same moment, all five were almost overcome by a smell so foul they wanted to vomit. The horror that followed will remain with them for the rest of their lives.

Two enormous gleaming eyes stared down at them. Thinking at first it might be a raccoon in a tree, they edged closer. But it was not a raccoon and there was no tree.

Picked out by the beam of Gene's torch was an enormous creature about 3 metres (10 feet) tall with a glistening red face and bulging eyes set at least a foot apart.

Rooted to the spot with terror, they all watched as the thing turned green and began to lumber towards them, hissing menacingly.

It was Kathleen who forced herself to move first.

Grabbing her boys and shouting at Gene to follow, she started to run down the hill as fast as her legs would carry her, dragging her children with her.

It was only after she had called the local sheriff that she noticed her sons' faces were now covered in smelly slime and their throats had started to swell.

The sheriff came but he was unable to carry out a full

investigation as his dogs refused to go anywhere near the spot where the monster had been seen. Then, not long after sunrise, a strange machine was seen taking off from the hilltop, and later the grass where it had rested was found to have been flattened.

Gene became seriously ill. Like the boys, his throat was badly inflamed and swollen and he also suffered from violent convulsions. Later, his symptoms were found to be identical to those of soldiers exposed to mustard gas during World War II.

If the story of a monster from outer space roaming the hills of West Virginia is incredible, then so too is the official explanation given out by the US Air Force.

They said that there was no UFO. What had been seen streaking through the sky that night was just a meteor. It had not landed at all, but only appeared to come down as it flashed over the summit of the hill.

There were no glowing eyes. What had first rooted Kathleen and the others to the spot was an owl, and its eyes had merely reflected the light of Guardsman Lemon's torch.

There was no monster. That was an illusion caused by light shining on the undergrowth.

And the symptoms afflicting the three boys and Gene Lemon? The US Air Force put them down to shock.

Canary Islands, 1976: Dr Padron Leon was in a taxi on his way to visit a patient on Grand Canaria, the largest of the Canary Islands. Sitting in the back seat with him was the patient's son, Santiago del Pino, who had called the doctor out.

As the taxi rounded a bend in the dusty road, the driver jammed on the brakes so hard that Dr Leon and Santiago were almost thrown to the floor.

They were about to shout angrily at the driver when they saw why he had braked so suddenly.

Hovering just above the ground was a transparent globe about 11 metres (36 feet) in diameter. Inside they could clearly see two aliens who seemed to be standing at a control panel. They wore tight-fitting red overalls, black helmets and black gloves. The creatures appeared to be 3 metres (10.5 feet) tall.

The driver tried to call for help but the car radio was dead. The three men started to shiver, not from fear but because they felt as if they were being bombarded by blast after blast of icy wind.

They found it hard enough to believe what they were seeing, but it was even harder to believe what happened next. Without warning, the globe started to get bigger and bigger and bigger, and when it was about the size of a twenty-storey building, it floated up in the air, and then vanished.

Dr Leon and his two companions ran to the nearest house where they found the owner and his wife clutching each other in terror. They too had seen the mysterious globe when they went to their window to see if there was any obvious reason why their television had suddenly gone blank.

EYEWITNESS

In 1992 Lise Milner, a vivacious young student, was sharing an apartment in San Francisco with a room mate, John. He was great fun; weird but great fun.

He used to make Lise laugh a lot and one night when he told her that he had been abducted by aliens, she thought it was a great joke. 'It's happened not just once, you know. I've been abducted lots of times. They follow me from city to city,' he said. 'Honestly, they do,' he went on, seeing Lise was starting to giggle. 'I wake up at night to find a bright light in the room and it slowly materializes into alien form. It's happened here, in this apartment.'

'Yeah!' Lise laughed. 'Tell that to the marines.'

Three weeks later, a friend came to stay. The three had a great evening before John decided to turn in for the night, and a couple of hours after that, Lise and her friend went to bed, too.

Lise woke up with a start in the middle of the night and was horrified to see bright lights, incredibly bright lights, shining through the dark curtains drawn across the bay windows. 'The lights,' she yelled, nudging her friend who was asleep beside her.

'What lights,' she yawned, raising herself onto one elbow and staring round her.

'There,' cried Lise, pointing at the window. 'Beyond the curtains.'

'You've been having a bad dream,' her friend sighed sleepily, rolled over and went back to sleep, leaving Lise staring at the lights.

She looked at her watch and saw it was 2.00 a.m.

Next morning Lise let her friend sleep in and went to the kitchen to fix herself some breakfast. John was there drinking coffee. 'Remember I told you about being abducted?' he said.

Lise nodded.

'It happened again last night,' he told her.

'What time?' Her voice must have been little more than a whisper, for she had to repeat her question.

'About two o'clock this morning,' came the reply.

'It was you, wasn't it?' Lise cried. 'Shining searchlights through my bedroom window? Through the curtains?'

John looked at her oddly. 'Lise,' he said, 'how could anyone shine searchlights through your window? You're on the top floor and your curtains are real thick as far as I recall. Nothing could shine through them.'

John moved on shortly afterwards. Lise and he still keep in touch though, and when he tells her that he's been abducted again, she doesn't laugh down the phone!

THE MYSTERY OF DREAMLAND

It's called Dreamland, or Area 51, and it's somewhere inside the USAF Groom Lake Air Base, a few kilometres outside the small town of Rachel in Nevada. Every night in the area around Dreamland, men and woman of all ages sit, binoculars and telescopes at the ready, hoping to catch sight of an alien spacecraft because for years UFO enthusiasts have reported mysterious lights moving incredibly fast, stopping dead in their tracks and then shooting off at mindbending speeds well beyond the capabilities of any known aircraft.

Not so long ago, the UFO spotters could get a good view of the area from the Freedom Mountain range nearby. But the US government spent millions of dollars buying up land for kilometres around and banning non-authorised personnel from it.

Odd, when according to the US government there is nothing special about Area 51.

'Nonsense', says aeronautics expert Bob Lazar who claims that between 1988 and 1989, he was one of many skilled men and women employed to examine crashed alien aircraft, to work out how they are powered and how any knowledge gleaned about them could be applied to the United States' space programme.

Lazar is adamant that he worked on nine alien spacecraft that had crash-landed and whose wreckage was stored in vast hangars cut into the mountain side.

'Lazar is a crank', says the US government. 'There is no top-secret base at Area 51.'

If that's true, why are there signposts on every track leading into the area, warning people to keep away?

Why is anyone who is caught having accidentally strayed into the area, arrested and jailed by the local sheriff for the night before being bussed back to Rachel?

Why is the area surrounded by powerful cameras that can read a car number plate from far away?

And if there is no top-secret base at Area 51, why have Russian satellite cameras photographed a 9.0 kilometre (6 mile) long runway there?

People who scoff at the existence of UFOs shake their heads and say knowingly, 'Everyone is aware that the Americans are developing stealth bombers and other new-generation aircraft at Dreamland.'

But that doesn't convince the army of UFO spotters who get as near as they can to watch the lights which they are convinced are damaged alien spacecraft, now repaired and being put through their paces with US Air Force pilots at the controls!

EYEWITNESS

In June 1957 Wendy Darden enlisted in the Woman's Army Corps and was stationed in Alabama, at Fort McClellan. On her first day there she noticed a girl who reminded her very much of herself, a kindred spirit who, like her, seemed to be something of a loner.

Later, as she prepared her space in the barracks, she felt a strange presence behind her, nothing threatening, in fact quite the opposite. She turned and saw the girl she had spotted earlier standing behind her. 'You believe in flying saucers, don't you?' the girl said.

Wendy was amazed, for two years before, her sister Pattie and she had seen a huge flying saucer in the sky above a shopping mall in Tracy, California, where they lived. No one else seemed to have noticed the twelve-metre diameter UFO skimming above the trees and hovering there for three or four minutes. But Wendy knew what she had seen and since then she had spotted UFOs several times in the sky above Tracy, flying in V-shaped formation over the town.

'How on earth do you know that?' Wendy asked her.

The girl smiled and said, 'I know many things.'

She told Wendy that her name was Audrey and that her home was in Washington State, on the northwest coast of the United States where her father was a UFO researcher.

From that day on, Wendy became firm friends with the tall, beautiful blonde with huge, saucer-shaped blue eyes. During their spare time Audrey taught Wendy about life in other worlds, in other galaxies. Often it was hard for Wendy to get her head round what she was being told, it all seemed so strange, but no matter, she couldn't listen to enough and their teacher/pupil sessions usually broke up with Wendy pleading with her friend not to stop.

Audrey was telepathic and could tell what Wendy was thinking often before she realized it herself. She never laughed at Audrey or scoffed at what she said, no matter how far-fetched it seemed.

One day when they were in the recreation room, Wendy noticed for the first time that Audrey had exceptionally beautiful hands with long, long fingers. Audrey saw her staring at the ridge that stuck out sideways from the side of each of her little fingers.

'What are these bumps on your hands?' Wendy asked.

'I was born with six fingers,' Audrey replied and went on to explain that she was from another planet. She and her family had been sent to Earth on a mission to help the people here to become more attuned to their inner selves and to be much less concerned with material wealth.

'The only physical difference between my race and yours is that we have six fingers on each hand,' Audrey said. 'The extra ones were removed surgically before we left our home planet, so that there would be nothing to give us away.'

Audrey was posted to another part of the States not long afterwards, but Wendy never forgot her. When she left the army she went to university where she studied Eastern religions and used much of what Audrey had taught her in the essays she had to write.

'I'm an ordained minister now,' Wendy said, 'and I help people who have been abducted by aliens to come to terms with their experience.

'I will always be grateful to Audrey, an alien from another planet, who helped me to decide what I really wanted to do with my life, and I'm certain we will meet again.'

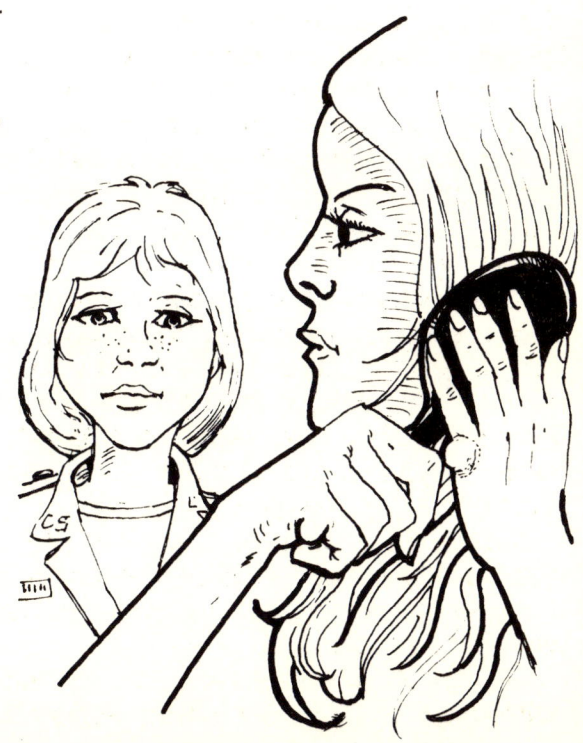

SPOOK FILES ENCYCLOPAEDIA

CLOSE ENCOUNTERS OF THE SECOND KIND

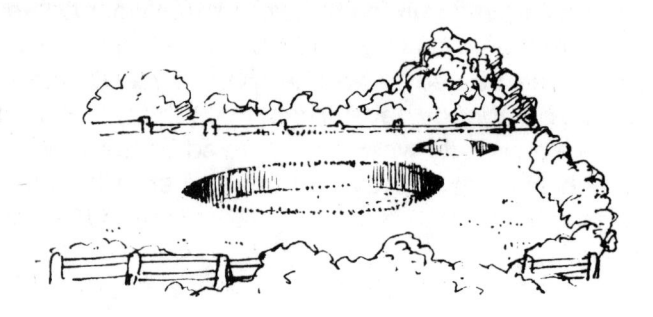

In a Close Encounter of the Second Kind, a UFO leaves behind physical evidence such as was found by Diane Messing and her daughter in Raeford, North Carolina.

It was just after midnight in June 1992 when the Messings' trailer home suddenly shook and rattled violently. It felt, and sounded, Diane said later, as if a freight train was hurtling by.

Nothing odd about that, you may say. But the trailer was nowhere near a railway line!

Startled, the two women rushed out to find the trailer's outside lights were off and the whole area around was bathed in a spooky red glow. What they took to be a fire was burning in a hayfield about 90 metres (300 feet) away.

But it wasn't a fire, they soon realized. The red light came from a glowing sphere about 4.5 metres (15 feet) across which was hovering silently above the hayfield.

They called the local sheriff's office straightaway, but by the time they got outside again, the sphere had vanished, and when the sheriff's men arrived, the trailer's lights were on again.

Next morning the two women walked over to the field and found that the spot where they had seen the glowing sphere had been flattened, with a scorched patch of grass that looked as if it had been combed into a swirling pattern.

Naturally, in a small town like Raeford, the story spread like wildfire and soon the area was packed with people who had come to see the strange markings. Among them was a mysterious man in black whose curious questions and weird manner made Mrs Messing shudder and her flesh creep.

Not only had the Messing women had a Close Encounter of the Second Kind, they had also met one of the mysterious men in black whose existence is denied by the US government, but who seem to appear with alarming frequency after a UFO has been seen or an alien encountered.

Here's a selection of COSKs from the UFO files.

England, December 1980: It was 3.00 a.m. when a radar at operator RAF Watton in Suffolk picked up something flying west over the North Sea. A check on the records later showed that just as it vanished from the Watton screens, it was seen by two security guards on duty at RAF Woodbridge, which at that time was leased to the USAF.

The men reported seeing lights drop from the sky into the trees of nearby Rendlesham Forest, and were given permission to leave their posts to investigate.

They jumped into a jeep, but had to abandon it and continue on foot once they were in the forest.

Eventually they saw it. Hovering above a clearing was a 2 metre (6 foot) high triangular cone about 3 metres (10 feet) across at the base. There was a flashing red light at the tip, and the base was lit up by a line of blue lights. The cone itself emitted a dazzling white light that illuminated the whole area.

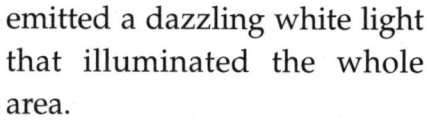

As the men approached, the cone took off and quickly flew out of sight. Convinced that they had seen a UFO, the men returned to the base to relate their story to an incredulous audience. But next day there were reports that at the same time as the sighting in the forest, animals in nearby farms had gone berserk.

Investigators were persuaded to examine the area and found indentations in the ground suggesting that rather than hovering, the UFO had been balancing on legs.

There were no tracks leading to these marks.

Many people thought that the security guards were responsible for them, but under very rigorous questioning, both men denied this.

To this day, there has never been a satisfactory explanation of the close encounter in Rendlesham Forest.

Finland, July 1981: It was a fairly windy evening and locals said that the sea currents were running strongly. Nevertheless two Finnish holidaymakers, enjoying a break at Cape Vaaraniemi on one of the hundreds of lakes in the middle of the country, decided to take out their hired motor launch.

It was just after 8.30 p.m. when they headed for home at full speed. Suddenly they saw a large sphere glowing in the sky, surrounded by one large and several smaller lights.

Terrified, they watched the large light close in on them. It was frighteningly close and they were making no headway, so they decided to switch off the engines and just wait in the hope that the light would soon disappear.

But it didn't disappear. It lingered overhead, and then a small black UFO appeared from nowhere and landed in the stern of their boat.

The boat was at once shrouded in a dense fog and one man was completely paralysed – not by fear, but because he was physically unable to move anything but his lips.

Then, as suddenly as it had appeared, the UFO disappeared again. The fog lifted, and with it went the paralysis.

But now the men found themselves sitting in different positions in the boat, and when they checked their watches, expecting about fifteen minutes to have passed, they discovered that it was now 4.10 in the morning.

They had been held captive by the alien UFO for over seven hours!

What was the physical evidence that makes this a close encounter of the second kind?

Ever since then, both men have suffered from hideous nightmares, have had difficulty in keeping their balance, and have often found themselves shaking uncontrollably for hours on end.

Kazakhstan, June 1982: The site of many of the USSR's rocket launches, Baikonur Cosmodrome had to be shut down for two weeks for repairs after this close encounter. It was on June 1 that two scientists working on putting Russia's space shuttle into orbit reported two UFOs flying overhead.

As they watched, one of the UFOs closed in on the launch pad while the other moved in on the staff's living quarters. Both hovered there briefly and then vanished.

Later, it was found that the welded joints on the launch

pad had been split and hundreds of rivets were missing. And at the staff block, all the windows had been shattered.

Cover up for a rocket launch that went wrong? Or aliens from another world trying to prevent man stepping into space?

Who can tell?

Turkmenistan, May 1990: Turkmenistan, formerly part of the USSR, borders on Afghanistan where, at the time of the encounter, a vicious war raged against Russian troops on active service there, backed by the Soviet 12 Air Defence Army which controlled Turkmenistan air space.

When an enormous orange UFO, judged to be 300 metres (1000 feet) in diameter was spotted over the area, the local air defence division sprang into action. Within minutes three SAM missiles were hurtling towards it.

The missiles never reached their target.

As they approached, three beams of light shot out from the UFO and blasted them from the sky.

Next, two jet fighters were sent up, but as they closed in, they met the same fate as the SAMs; the planes crashed to the ground 900 metres (3000 feet) below, killing everyone.

The authorities later denied that the incident had ever occurred.

Eyewitnesses know what they saw.

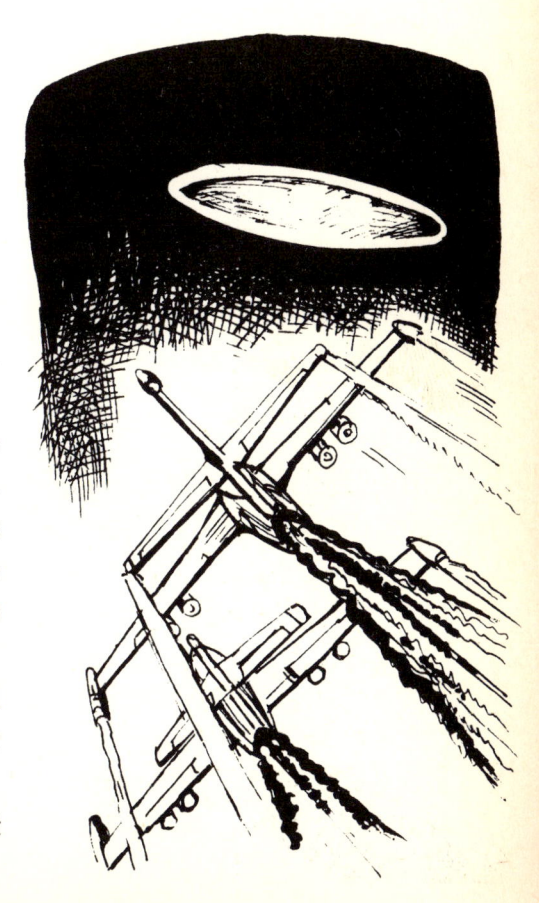

A CLOSE ENCOUNTER OF THE MOST TRAGIC KIND

On July 17, 1996, TWA Flight 800 took off from New York's Kennedy Airport on a routine flight for Paris. A few minutes later, it exploded in mid-air off Long Island and plunged into the ocean thousands of metres below, killing everyone on board.

Experts who raced to the scene reckon that the back half of the plane carried on flying for at least a minute after the explosion, causing unimaginable terror to passengers still strapped into their seats and who had not been sucked out into the black void beyond.

Piece by piece the wreckage was recovered from the water and reassembled as far as possible in a huge hangar near New York. The same experts examined each fragment, searching for any shred of evidence as to what had caused the plane to blow up.

Eventually the cause was identified as an explosion in one of the fuel tanks.

But no one knows what caused that explosion.

Some people believe it was a terrorist bomb. So far, no evidence has been found for that theory, and usually after a terrorist outrage, those responsible issue a statement saying they did it. No such statement has ever been issued.

Others believe the explosion was caused by a stray missile accidentally fired from an American submarine or air base. A painstaking check of military records has shown that this is not the case.

There is a third theory. Just before the explosion, several eyewitnesses reported seeing a white light streaking towards the doomed aircraft. Could TWA Flight 800 have collided with a UFO?

UNIDENTIFIED SUBMERSIBLE OBJECTS

Alien-powered vehicles are not necessarily flying objects; there have been many reports from around the world of Unidentified Submersible Objects (USOs)...

Tierra del Fuego, Argentina, June 1950: Romero Ernesto Suarez was enjoying an evening stroll along the coast road that runs between Rio Grande and San Sebastian in the remote part of the world that lies at the tip of South America when a crashing sound coming from somewhere at sea stopped him in his tracks, for it was a calm night with little wind.

Romero screwed up his eyes, peered into the gathering darkness and saw something emerge from the sea about 500 metres from the coast. The enormous, glowing, oval-shaped object rose vertically into the sky and when it was about three or four hundred metres above the water, turned a sharp 90 degree angle, shot off to the northwest and vanished a few seconds later.

Fifteen days later, on another part of the coast, Romero saw more USOs, this time four small discs which shot from beneath the waves in perfect formation, then flew along the coastline before disappearing from view in the blink of an eye.

The Gulf of Genoa, June 1961: Four young Italians were enjoying an early morning cruise in a motor boat off the town of Savona when suddenly the water turned from almost dead calm to very choppy, and the boat began to roll wildly. The men looked round, expecting to see that they had strayed into the wake of a tanker or some other large vessel.

What they saw was no ship. About a kilometre away, the water was bulging like an enormous ball. As they stared at it, wondering what on earth was happening, a 'strange contraption' rose from the bulge. As it emerged from the waves, the sea became choppier and choppier and at one point the four thought they were about to be thrown overboard.

A few moments later the contraption was completely out of the water and when it was about ten metres above the waves, it hovered in the air for a few seconds, rocking gently from side to side before a halo formed round its base and it sped across the sea, vanishing from sight a second or two later.

Le Brusc, France, August, 1962: Even now, none of the three fishermen who witnessed a USO very early one moonlit morning as their small fishing boats bobbed about in the water off a small fishing village on the French Riviera, are willing to have their names published, so scared are they at what they saw.

Three hundred metres from where they had dropped their nets, something which they took to be a small submarine rose from the sea. As they watched, about a dozen frogmen appeared from the sea and clambered onto it. Then, one by one the frogmen clambered up the metal foot- and handholds on the outside of the turret in the middle of the deck and disappeared into it.

One of the fishermen shouted a friendly greeting, which the frogmen ignored until the last of them turned and waved when he was half-way up the turret, then squeezed himself into it and vanished.

'That's something to tell the children when we get back to Le Brusc,' said one of the men. 'Seeing a foreign submarine and frogmen so close to the shore."

The words were hardly out of his mouth before the 'submarine' rose out of the water and hung in the air just above the waves. A beam of white light shot from the craft, catching the fishing boats in its glare. Then, as suddenly as it had appeared, the light went out. Seconds later, the craft began to glow orange and started to rotate very slowly, rising in the air until it was twenty metres above the water.

The dumbfounded fishermen could now see that the craft was shaped like a spinning-top which started to spin faster and faster before it began to glow red and shot off horizontally towards the open sea, like a dazzling fireball.

Just when it looked as if it was about to vanish from view, it boomeranged back, gained height and rose so rapidly into the sky that a second later it was little more than a pinprick of light, soon lost among the stars.

As one of the fishermen is reported to have said later, 'What was really eerie was not just the thing itself, but the absolute silence with which it moved. All we could hear was the waves lapping against the boat, even when it was spinning at its fastest.'

The Atlantic Ocean, July 1967: The officers and crew of the Argentinian steamer Naviero, cruising 190 kilometres off the coast of Brazil, were enjoying their supper when the officer on watch buzzed the captain, Julian Lucas Ardanza, to tell him that the ship was being shadowed by an unknown craft of some sort.

Captain Ardanza made his way to the deck where he could plainly see a shining, cigar-shaped object about 16 metres his ship. It looked to be at most 30 metres long, and was moving through the water without making any noise whatsoever or creating any wake.

'A submarine of some kind,' one of the other officers suggested. But there was no sign of a periscope, conning tower or the railings with which most, if not all, submarines are fitted.

For fifteen minutes the curious craft followed Naviero before it started to glow orange-red, submerged and plunged downwards out of sight.

George Adamski, an American who claimed to have been in contact with aliens many times, says he was told by his out-of-this-world friends that the crew of the USO seen by Captain Ardanza and others aboard Naviero were studying the bottom of the Atlantic Ocean off the coast of South America in 1967 as it was one of the few areas of the Earth they had not yet charted.

They would, Adamski went on, have liked to surface to make themselves known but were scared of the hostility they might encounter.

AND FOR A LAST CLOSE ENCOUNTER OF THE SECOND KIND . . .

New Mexico, July 1947: Farmer William 'Mac' Brazel was used to seeing curious objects in the sky and hearing the occasional explosion, for he lived not far from the United States atom bomb and missile test bases at White Sands and the Alamogordo/Holloman air base.

But the explosion he heard that thundery night in July was unlike anything he had ever heard before.

Next day, Mac and a friend rode out to investigate, and to make sure his sheep had come to no harm.

A few kilometres from the farmhouse the two men, to their horror, came across what looked like pieces of a wrecked aircraft scattered over an area a kilometre wide.

In the centre of the wreckage was a great hole in the ground with a deep furrow running out from it. Obviously, the men thought, the aircraft had gone out of control and then skidded on impact with the ground.

But when Mac picked up a piece of the wreckage, he was astonished by its lightness. And when he bent it, it sprang back to its original shape as soon as he let go.

Other pieces of debris looked like balsa wood, but when Mac tried to burn it, it would not catch fire.

After showing samples of their find to family and friends, the two men took them to the police in Roswell, the nearest town.

The sheriff immediately sent two of his deputies to the site which was 13 kilometres (8 miles) away and told Mac to pay a visit to the air base and show the military what he had found.

Three officers from the base drove out to the area, loaded some of the debris onto their truck and returned to base.

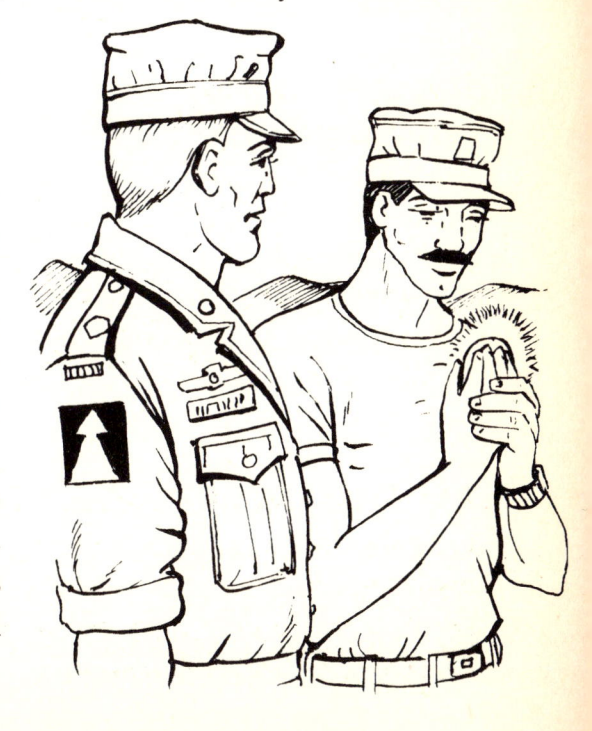

They also collected Mac, who they held in custody for a whole week before releasing him.

Meanwhile, the area was cordoned off and much of the debris collected, crated and flown to Dayton, Ohio. There are still some people who remember that, although the crates were packed tight, they were quite light and each one could be lifted easily by one man.

That wasn't all that was found near Roswell around that time.

Civil engineer Grady L. Barnett saw something glistening on the ground one day while working for the Soil Conservation Service in the desert about 5 kilometres (3 miles) from where Mac Brazel had come across the strange wreckage.

From a distance he thought it might be a small aircraft that had crashed, but as he came closer he saw it was a metallic disc, about 9 metres (30 feet) in diameter.

Coming closer still, he was horrified to find that the disc was surrounded by small, hairless, humanoid creatures wearing grey, one-piece suits.

There were more of the little men inside the disc – and they were all dead.

He was still trying to convince himself that he had not walked into an alien nightmare when a group of students on an archaeological dig turned up and as they all stood gazing in open-mouthed astonishment, officers and soldiers from the air base arrived in a jeep, promptly declared the area out of bounds to civilians, and warned everyone to keep their mouths shut.

Grady was so stricken by the experience that for three years he didn't say a word.

And the archaeological students must have been even worse affected, for none of them has ever come forward.

Many think that Grady Barnett had been overcome by the

heat of the desert sun and had imagined everything he saw.

But others are convinced that in July 1947, an alien spacecraft somehow went wrong and disintegrated in the air above the New Mexican desert, and what Grady found was the main body of a UFO and the dead creatures its crew.

And they believe that what was found was stored in Hangar 18 at the Wright Patterson air force base at Dayton, Ohio, before being moved to a remote air base, 320 kilometres (200 miles) north of Las Vegas.

The US government is adamant that this is not true.

But think. The US president, Richard Nixon, denied being involved in the cover-up of a bungled break-in in Washington in the mid-1970s, and he resigned when it turned out he was lying.

So if you can't trust a president to tell the truth, who can you trust?

Grady Barnett swears that he saw dead aliens. Had they been alive, he would have been one of many who have had a close encounter of the third kind. As it is, his story belongs with those encounters of the second kind.

As for Mac Brazel's find, the official story is that the wreckage was that of an experimental weather balloon.

THE BLUE ROOM

Many people believe that deep within the US Wright Patterson Airport Base at Dayton, Ohio, is a storehouse where the US government keep UFOs that have crashed on Earth and the remains of aliens trapped inside them. The base, it is claimed, is also the headquarters of a top-secret 'quick reaction force' whose job it is to retrieve downed UFOs.

Only top-ranking officials and high-ranking visitors are permitted to enter the alien museum and are sworn to secrecy before entering.

One high-ranking American who tried to gain access was Senator Barry Goldwater, one of the United States' leading politicians of the 1960s and a former presidential candidate. Later he wrote, 'The subject of UFOs having interested me for some time, I made an effort to find out what is in Wright Patterson, but it is still classified above top secret.'

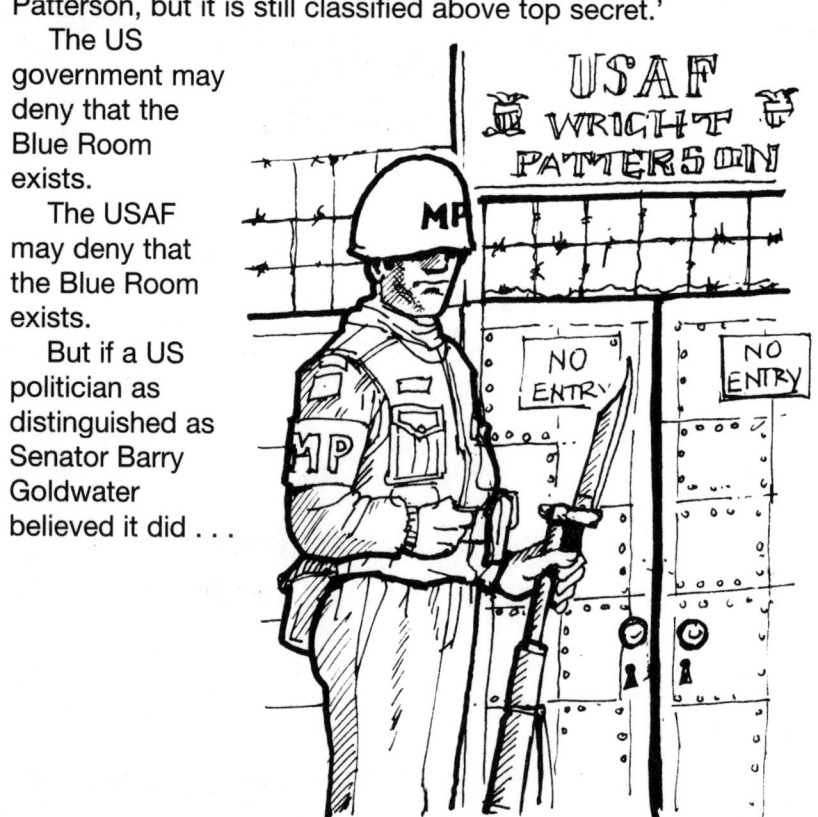

The US government may deny that the Blue Room exists.

The USAF may deny that the Blue Room exists.

But if a US politician as distinguished as Senator Barry Goldwater believed it did . . .

SPOOK FILES ENCYCLOPAEDIA

CLOSE ENCOUNTERS OF THE THIRD KIND

**Look out! Look out!
There are Aliens about!**

ALIENS UNDERGROUND

Some people believe that the Earth is hollow, and that aliens live deep below the surface. Cranks, you may say, especially when you hear the tale that Richard Byrd, an American who claimed to have met these subterranean aliens, had to tell.

In 1947, he set off from an air base in the Arctic Circle to fly over the North Pole. He had been in the air for three hours when, glancing down, he noticed he was flying over a large area of yellow ice.

Flying lower, he saw that the ice was dotted with patches of red and purple.

Then he was astonished to find that he was flying over a range of mountains that appeared in none of the maps that had been made of the area.

As he flew over them he was horrified to find that the controls of his plane refused to respond and the plane seemed to be floating on a cushion of air.

Gazing around him in panic, he could hardly believe his eyes when he saw that he was heading for a green valley. Suddenly he saw a plane flying alongside him and a voice crackled over his radio. 'Welcome to our domain. We shall land you in exactly seven minutes,' the voice said. And then, as if sensing the pilot's fear, went on, 'Relax. You are in good hands.'

Byrd was powerless to prevent his plane being landed alongside his escort.

He was helped out of the cockpit and led underground into what he described as a huge, shimmering city inhabited by very tall, blond humanoids.

Curiously, he felt no fear as he was taken into a beautiful underground chamber where the aliens' leader, the Master, was waiting to greet him.

Byrd listened in amazement as the Master told him that he

and the others belonged to a race called the Arianni, who had lived in the bowels of the Earth for centuries. They had never troubled the human race until now and had only decided to make their presence known because they were concerned that underground nuclear testing would contaminate their subterranean world.

The Master went on to say that the Arianni had tried to contact other humans apart from Byrd, to tell them how concerned they were. But their warnings were being ignored and the aircraft they travelled in when above ground – he called them 'Fugelrads' – had been fired at.

Just before Byrd was led back to his plane, the Master warned him that the world would come to an end within a hundred years. Not all humans would die, though. And when the dust had settled, the Arianni would come to the surface to help the survivors start to rebuild a peaceful, well-ordered society in which they and human beings could live side by side.

Byrd was told to warn the human race what lay in store for them when he returned to base, and later he passed the message on to President Truman. He, in turn, must have passed it on to the Pentagon, for shortly afterwards Byrd was approached by military top brass who swore him to secrecy.

The story only came to light when Byrd died and the diary in which he had written down details of his experience was found among his papers.

A crank's tale? Richard B. Byrd was no crank. He had been a Rear Admiral in the US Navy, was the first man to fly over the North Pole, in 1926, and one of the foremost polar explorers of his generation.

EYEWITNESS

According to eyewitnesses, the UFO was a disc with a diameter of between one hundred and two hundred metres. Two pulsating lights were positioned on its sides. When the object flew in a horizontal plane, the line of the lights was parallel to the horizon. During vertical movement it rotated and was perpendicular to the ground. Moreover, the object rotated around its axis and performed an 'S-turn' flight, both in the horizontal and vertical planes.

Next, the UFO hovered above the ground and then flew with a speed exceeding that of the modern-day jet fighter by two or three times. All of the observers noticed that the flight speed was directly related to the flashing of the side lights. The more often they flashed, the higher the speed.

GENERAL IGOR MALTSEV, USSR AIR DEFENCE FORCES.

EYEWITNESS

It was late one night in 1982. Elizabeth Merrit, a Suffolk housewife, had just driven through a seemingly deserted small town and was approaching a junction in the road.

As she slowed down, she was astonished to see three bright white beams of light coming straight down from the sky. 'There was no shape behind the lights, they seemed to be in a triangle,' she wrote later, 'but not particularly symmetrical. I couldn't believe it.'

Elizabeth stopped her car, turned off the radio, and opened the car door, but there was nothing to be heard. Thinking her imagination must be playing tricks on her, she turned the ignition key, drove to the junction and turned right.

'After that, it's a straight road. And this contraption followed me up it' she said. 'I could see the bright lights moving along in the rear mirror.'

By now, her heart was absolutely thumping. 'I admit I wasn't very brave - I was really shaking. Then this thing veered off to the right – and the lights were gone.'

Elizabeth had always scoffed at people, who claim to have seen UFOs.

Not any more!

California, USA, 1952: Hamburger-bar assistant, George Adamski, had always been convinced that the planets in our solar system are inhabited, and when he heard a rumour that a flying saucer had landed in the desert not far from where he worked, he and some friends set off to find it.

As they were enjoying a picnic lunch, they saw floating above them what Adamski later described as, 'a gigantic cigar-shaped silvery ship without wings.'

Anxious to see whether it would land, Adamski and two of his companions followed it, driving further and further into the desert.

The two friends soon tired of their chase and went home, leaving Adamski alone.

When he returned some time later he had an amazing story to tell. A spacecraft had appeared and, as Adamski came closer, he saw a figure waving at him from the mouth of a ravine. It seemed to be beckoning him on, and as he approached, Adamski knew without a doubt that it was an alien.

'It was one of the most beautiful things I have ever seen,' he said, and went on to describe it in detail. It was about 1.5 metres (5.5 feet) tall and of medium build. Its wavy fair hair fell to its shoulders and slanting grey eyes shone in its suntanned face. Its cheekbones were high and its nose finely chiselled.

The alien wore a one-piece, high-collared brown garment with a broad waistband. Its square-toed shoes were the colour of blood.

The creature did not speak, but made gestures with its hands and at the same time gazed at Adamski so fixedly that he had no difficulty in understanding its message.

It had come from Venus, where the inhabitants were concerned that the Earth was in danger of destruction from the radioactive fallout from nuclear tests. It had come to see if these fears were justified.

Then the alien got back into its spacecraft which was waiting nearby, and then took off without a sound.

People laughed at Adamski's story, but one investigator who talked to him said he did not see why anyone should disbelieve him. 'He was one of the most lucid and intelligent men I have met.'

California, USA, 1953: Mary Cosway and Anne Frampton (not their real names) were two friends who shared a remote cabin on the edge of the Mojave Desert. They were terrified when one day in March a gang of bikers roared in a cloud of dust along the canyon where they lived.

After circling the cabin several times, laughing and jeering, the bikers rode off after the girls pleaded with them to stop.

At 2.00 a.m. Mary was woken up by a bright light outside the cabin. Scared that the bike gang had returned, she roused her roommate and the two of them looked out fearfully.

Suddenly Mary felt dizzy and disorientated and had to lie down. Recovering almost immediately, she looked at her bedside clock and saw to her astonishment that now it said 4.20 a.m.

Almost two-and-a-half hours had passed in what had seemed like minutes.

As soon as it was light, the two girls fled from their cabin and for several days were too scared to return.

Years passed without any further incident but Mary remained haunted by the certainty that her memory of that night was incomplete.

At last, in 1975, she decided to undergo hypnosis. As a result she finally recalled in detail what had happened to her and her friend Anne.

Something had made the girls leave the cabin and follow the light along the canyon. A UFO awaited them and they were wafted aboard and examined by scanning machines.

The examination over, small aliens clad in black appeared and communicated with the girls by telepathy, telling them not to be alarmed. They were then returned to their cabin.

At Mary's request, Anne had agreed to be hypnotized too, but sadly recalled nothing. But to this day, Mary is convinced that she had a close encounter of the third kind with aliens aboard their spaceship floating above a canyon in the Californian desert.

Croix d'Epine, France, 1954: Marcel Delatre, a nineteen-year-old motor mechanic, was riding home from work one night on his scooter when suddenly he had to jam on the brakes. A UFO had appeared from nowhere and landed in the road in front of him.

Moments later, what Marcel described as, 'potato bags,' waddled up to the UFO.

Summoning all his courage, he got off his scooter and ran towards the UFO to investigate. But as he got near it, the craft turned blue, rose in the air, and vanished.

Marcel thought he must have imagined the whole thing, but when he heard that two other people in nearby villages had reported seeing the UFO, he wasn't so sure.

Kentucky, August 1955: Billy Ray Taylor and his family were visiting friends. It was seven o'clock in the evening when Billy Ray's host, Elmer Sutton, asked him to fetch water from the well. As he lowered the bucket, he was distracted by a noise, and looking round saw something coming in to land in a hollow not far away. As it got closer to the ground, fumes of different colours shot out from the exhaust.

Billy Ray ran inside to tell the others what he had seen, but everyone thought he was joking, and the more he insisted, the more they laughed.

An hour later the dog began to howl. Thinking it might be intruders, Billy Ray and Elmer grabbed their guns and ran outside to scare them off.

Walking towards them was a small creature about 1 metre (3 feet) tall, with its hands held over its egg-shaped head. Large eyes, set wide apart, glowed yellow, and large ears flapped on either side of its head. Its slim body shone silver.

Billy Ray and Elmer didn't wait to find out who or what was approaching them. They took aim and fired.

The shots made the alien somersault backwards, but didn't kill it. Picking itself up, it scurried off. And even as it ran, more and more goblin-like creatures appeared, until the house was surrounded. There was even one on the roof. When it got hit by a bullet, it floated down and came to rest on a fence nearby. Billy Ray and Elmer fired again and it scampered off on all fours into a patch of weeds.

The entire yard soon crackled and flared with gunfire as the two men shot at alien after alien, but the bullets didn't kill them, just scared them off.

Their last shots fired, the two terrified men raced back to the relative safety of the house and locked all doors.

Just in time, for the little aliens were hot on their heels. They rattled the handles, peered through the windows and drummed on the roof.

Suddenly they vanished.

Billy Ray and Elmer waited for three hours, too scared to move, before hustling their wives and children into their cars and heading for Hopkinsville, the nearest town, about 11 kilometres (7 miles) away. There they reported the events of the night to the police.

The police chief and five of his men, accompanied by Billy Ray and Elmer, sped back to the Sutton farm. There was no sign of aliens and no sign of the spacecraft Billy Ray assured them he had seen coming in to land.

It was two o'clock in the morning when the police left, warning Billy Ray and Elmer not to waste police time in future.

But no sooner had they gone than the aliens reappeared and again the house was surrounded.

It was after five o'clock when they finally gave up and left.

The story soon got about and Billy Ray, Elmer and their families had to endure the mocking laughter of their neighbours every time they went into town. But they stuck to their story, and to this day, the children, now middle-aged, insist that they were held besieged at the Sutton place by a band of aliens that night in August 1955.

Minas Gerais, Brazil, 1957: A farmer's son, Antonio Villas Boas, was out ploughing a field one night in October when he saw what he described as a large red star in the sky.

It hovered briefly then floated down, landing 15 metres (50 feet) from Antonio's tractor, its brilliance far outshining his tractor's lights.

The UFO was egg-shaped with purple lights dotted round its rim. Above the lights, its top part spun round and round, and as it landed, the whole craft changed colour from red to green.

Antonio rammed the gearstick into drive, but he had travelled only a few metres before the tractor's engine came to a spluttering stop. He jumped down from the cab and started to run home across the freshly ploughed field. Seconds later he was overtaken by three aliens. Although he was at least a head taller than the creatures, they were too strong for him and dragged him off to the spacecraft where more aliens were waiting.

They were dressed in close-fitting grey suits and helmets, thick-soled shoes and clumsy looking gloves. Three tubes led from their helmets, one to each armpit and one to the small of the back. Through the helmets, small, piercing blue eyes stared at Antonio.

The aliens, speaking to each other in odd, barking tones, undressed Antonio and took a blood sample from him. He was then introduced to a beautiful alien woman before being given a guided tour of the spacecraft. He was then led back to his field.

But just before he left the spacecraft, the alien woman told Antonio she would have a baby and that he would be its father!

His family laughed at his story, but a few days later Antonio felt sick, then broke out in a curious rash. The doctor who examined him told him he was suffering from radiation sickness!

That, coupled with Antonio's reputation for being as honest as the day is long, convinced his family he had been telling the truth.

If so, perhaps somewhere out in space there is an alien with a human father!

Quaroubles, France, 1954: It was 10.30 p.m. when farmworker Marius Dewilde's dog started to howl. Stepping outside to investigate, Marius was stopped in his tracks at the sight of a pair of 2 metre (6.5 feet) tall shapes shuffling along on stumpy little legs. He was about to go forward for a closer look when a beam of light shot out from something sitting on the ground nearby, rooting him to the spot.

As the dog continued to howl, Marius blinked in amazement at what happened next. The source of the light took on the shape of a spacecraft, and as the two aliens beings entered it, the spacecraft glowed red, shot off and vanished in seconds.

Later, deep marks in the earth were examined by an engineers who estimated they had been made by something weighing at least thirty tonnes.

Marius wasn't the only one to have seen the UFO that night. Five other people reported it to the police, but Marius was the only one to have had such a close encounter with creatures from another world.

Wisconsin, USA, 1961: It was breakfast time when Joe Simonton, a sixty-year-old chicken farmer, looked out of his kitchen window and saw a silver object coming in to land in his yard.

Three-and-a-half metres (12 feet) high and 9 metres (30 feet) in diameter, it was shaped like two bowls stuck together at the rim with exhaust pipes fitted around the lip which, like the rest of the UFO, shone brighter than chrome.

By the time Joe had reached the yard, the spacecraft had landed. A hatch slid open and three aliens stepped out. The aliens looked like humans, around 1.5 metres (5 feet) tall, wearing black suits, dark poloneck sweaters and helmets that looked to Joe as though they had been knitted.

One alien then held out a jug to Joe and made hand gestures to explain that he wanted something to drink.

The terrified chicken farmer ran back to the house to fill the jug with water. When he got back, he could see another alien cooking inside the craft. He also noted that several instrument panels were set in the gleaming grey walls of the interior.

Joe gave the aliens the jug of water, and when he indicated that he would like something to eat in exchange, the alien chef passed him three of the pancakes he had been cooking.

The three aliens then re-entered the craft, closed the hatch and Joe watched as the spacecraft took off so fast a grove of pine trees was damaged in the blast.

Joe tried to eat one of the pancakes, but it tasted like cardboard and he put it aside with the other two. When he told his friends of his encounter, one of them, a judge and keen ufologist, asked him to send the pancakes off to be analysed.

The results were disappointing. The pancakes were made of everyday ingredients such as bran, soya beans and wheat, and the experts said that they must have been made on Earth.

But if you wanted to convince people you had some alien food in your larder, would you try to hoodwink experts with something so easily analysed?

Joe insists that what he saw really happened, and friends who had known him for years claimed he was not the sort of man to cook up a far-fetched tale about alien pancakes.

EYEWITNESS

Russell Virden was nine when his father, a master-sergeant in the Signal Corps, was transferred from a base in Texas to Hattiesburg in Mississippi where his parents were allocated the typically thin-walled quarters the army provided for married couples and their families.

It was November, 1943, and the Second World War was raging in Europe and the Far East, but in Mississippi it may as well have been being fought on the Moon for all the impact it had on the Russell and his brothers.

The boys had been put to bed that night and were sound asleep when they were awakened by their mother screaming, 'His face was green! His face was green,' over and over again.

Sergeant Virden was on duty so it was up to his sons to try to calm their mother.

'Whose face?' Russell's elder brother, Louis, kept asking her, but she just stared straight ahead, sobbing, 'His face was green!'

Suddenly they heard a shotgun being fired outside.

Everyone ran into the night and found their next-door neighbour, Sergeant Thorne, standing there, a still-smoking gun cradled in the nook of his elbow.

'I hit him,' he cried. 'I hit him but he just kept on running.'

'Hit who?' Louis asked.

'An intruder!' Sergeant Thorne replied, then said again, 'I hit him, but he just kept on running.'

Just then, another soldier, carrying a flashlight, appeared. When he heard what had happened, he shone the lamp on the path that led from the Virden's house to the highway not far away. It was splattered with a sticky yellow substance.

Whatever Mrs Virden had seen, it was no ordinary prowler.

If she was right, it had a green face.

If what Sergeant Thorne said was true, it had been able to run off despite having taken the full brunt of a 12-bore shotgun being fired at it.

And if what everyone saw on the path was what they thought it was, yellow blood coursed through its veins.

The boys were herded back into the house and hustled into

their bedroom, but because the walls were so thin they could hear their mother tell the two soldiers that she had been awakened a few minutes earlier by a loud hammering on the front door. She had gone to answer it but when she drew back the curtain to see who was there, there was no one.

A split second later, someone pounded on the back door, but again when she went to see what the commotion was all about, there was no one there and the knocking reverted to the front.

She dashed to the front door and jerked back the curtain. The face she saw was not a human one.

'It was an alien,' she sobbed. 'An alien with a green face.'

When the story spread around the base, most people thought Mrs Virden had been the victim of a late, cruel trick-or-treat hoax.

But no human Hallowe'en hoaxer could have carried on running after having been blasted by a powerful shotgun. And to the day she died, Russell's mother was convinced she had come face to face with a horrifying, green-faced, yellow-blooded being from another planet.

CLOSE ENCOUNTERS OF THE FOURTH KIND

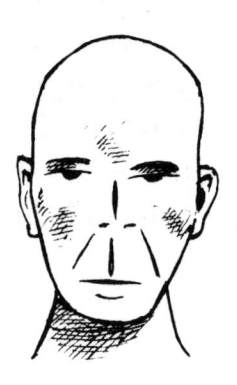

Some Close Encounters of the Fourth Kind are so terrifying, those who experience them are never quite the same again. Not surprising, for Close Encounters of the Fourth Kind are also called Alien Abductions. But sometimes they are not so scary, as some of the stories that follow show.

Argentina, 1975: Walter Carlos Diaz was walking home from his night job in Bahia Blanca early in the morning on January 4, when suddenly an ear-splitting whine filled his head. As he looked around to see where the noise was coming from, he was blinded by a dazzling light and the street under his feet started to vibrate.

When the light faded, he found himself suspended in the air, 3 metres (10 feet) above the pavement, whereupon he passed out.

The next thing he knew he was in a bright green dome, with three green-skinned aliens standing nearby. He felt no fear as they approached him and began to pull handfuls of hair from his head, but so gently that he felt no pain.

After blacking out again, he came to with a jolt and found he was lying by the roadside. His newspaper and the plastic bag holding his working clothes were neatly beside him.

He glanced at his watch and saw that four hours had passed since he had left work.

But he had no idea where he was.

He asked a passer-by, who eyed him suspiciously before telling him he was in Buenos Aires.

Buenos Aires is 800 kilometres (500 miles) from Bahia Blanca. No train service or flight could have got him there in four hours at that time in the morning.

His employers vouch for the fact that he left his workplace at the time he stated.

Hospital records in Buenos Aires prove that he was admitted just over four hours later!

Arizona, 1975: When Mike Rogers and his team of six foresters had finished work for the day, they stowed their equipment in their truck and headed for Snowflake, a small town nearby.

The truck was roaring up a hill when suddenly Mike slammed on the brakes, for hovering in the sky just ahead was a disc-shaped object, about 6 metres (20 feet) wide, 2.5 metres (8 feet) high and glowing a bright amber colour.

Six of the men in the truck froze in their seats.

The seventh, Travis Walton, a twenty-two-year-old logger, clambered out of the truck and walked towards the UFO.

Mike yelled at him to come back, but Travis walked on and, as he neared the UFO, he started to shake alarmingly.

Then a bolt of greenish-blue light shot from the UFO, struck Travis and threw him to the ground.

As he lay there bathed in the spooky light, his friends were about to go and help him, but without warning or explanation, Mike rammed his foot on the accelerator and the truck tore on up the hill.

Mike didn't stop until the truck screeched to a halt outside the sheriff's office in Snowflake where the six terrified foresters told the lawman what had happened.

Sheriff Ellison organized a full-scale search party to return to the woods to search for Travis.

Three of Mike's men, too scared to return to the forest, refused to join in the search.

The others, along with more men from Snowflake, spread out and roamed the forest calling out Travis's name, but there was no sign of the young woodsman.

The search party returned to the forest the next day and the day after that, but they still found nothing.

Sheriff Ellison called Mike and the five others into his office and angrily accused them of killing Travis, hiding the body and making up a cock-and-bull story about a UFO to cover their tracks.

The men vigorously denied it, insisting that what they had reported was the truth. And then one of the men started to cry, repeating over and over again through his tears that there had been a UFO and Travis really had been hit by a beam of blue light.

'Why didn't you go and help him?' asked the sheriff.

'Too scared,' came the reply.

Eventually Sheriff Ellison found it hard to believe that the men were lying, or if they were, they were the most convincing liars he had ever come across.

The men agreed to take a lie detector test and even though they knew they had been telling the truth, were relieved when the tests backed them up.

Six days after Travis vanished, his sister was awoken by her telephone ringing.

When she picked up the receiver she was overjoyed to hear Travis's voice on the other end of the line.

'Where are you?' she asked. 'Where have you been?'

Travis sounded dazed and confused, but eventually he calmed down and told his sister that he was in a call box just outside Snowflake, 20 kilometres (12.5 miles) from where she and the rest of Travis's family lived.

As soon as Travis's brother heard where the missing lad was, he jumped into his car and sped off towards Snowflake.

When he reached the call box, he found a wild-eyed,

exhausted Travis huddled beside it. Helping his brother into the car, he drove him home with all speed.

Soon the dazed Travis was cowering on a sofa as his sister bombarded him with questions.

At first he said nothing, but eventually in a voice so quiet it was hard to understand what he was saying, he began to tell his story.

The moment the beam of light had struck him, he had lost consciousness. When he came to, he found himself lying on a table in a brightly lit room.

'I thought at first Mike must have driven me to the hospital,' he said, his voice shaking, 'so I called for a nurse.'

But no nurse answered his call.

Instead, the blood froze in his veins when three alien faces appeared and stared down at him. Completely bald, the creatures had huge, slanting eyes and tiny, slit-like mouths.

Travis jumped down from the table and, grabbing the first thing that came to hand – a transparent glass tube – swung it desperately at the aliens.

The terrifying trio scuttled off, leaving Travis alone.

He tore from the room and sprinted along a corridor, through another door and found himself at a window gazing down on the Earth, a blue ball hundreds of kilometres below.

Even as he looked, the planet got smaller and smaller, until it was just a pinprick of light in a galaxy of stars.

Suddenly Travis knew he wasn't alone.

He spun round and found himself face to face with a human-like figure, its head encased in a glass dome.

It turned away, beckoning Travis to follow.

A minute or two later, Travis was standing in a vast hangar, where tall, fair-haired aliens with golden eyes were working on flying saucers of various sizes.

Desperate to know what was happening and where he was, Travis began to question the alien he had followed. Ignoring the questions, it told him to lie down.

He thought of trying to run, but where to? So he obeyed the order.

No sooner was he on his back than a mask was put over his face, and the next thing he knew he was back on Earth.

A roaring sound above his head made him look up and he saw the UFO streak off in a blast of heat that almost threw him to the ground.

Dazed and totally bewildered, he gradually recovered enough to realize he was on the highway leading to Snowflake, and eventually was able to stumble along until he reached the call box.

It is only fair to mention certain facts about Travis and his fellow foresters.

(1) Mike and the others were behind with the work they were contracted to do. Autumn was turning to winter and there was no way they could have finished the job before snow made it impossible to continue. Had they made up the story as a distraction?

(2) Travis Walton had been in trouble with the police and was a well-known practical joker. He was also passionately interested in UFOs and had read book after book about them.

(3) His mother did not seem unduly worried by her son's disappearance. Was she involved in an elaborate hoax dreamed up by Travis?

But Travis had been

missing for days. His disappearance was given wide publicity, and no one came forward to say they had seen him during that time.

The others refused to change a word of their story, despite being offered large sums of money from newspapers to admit that it had all been a hoax.

And to this day, Travis Walton insists he was taken aboard an alien spacecraft and taken for a trip around the stars.

Brazil, 1980: Luli Oswald, a Brazilian concert pianist, and a friend were driving along the coast road south of Rio de Janeiro when they saw something emerge from the ocean. Some things rather, for as they stared, a fleet of strange craft broke through the waves, 'like mushrooms with water spilling over them,' was how Luli later described them to the police. 'Then we noticed a big black one ahead of us. It seemed to be about 100 metres (330 feet) across with a small dome on top.'

Luli's friend, Fauze Mehlen, who was at the wheel, lost control of the car which weaved wildly across the road with the doors flying open and then slamming shut as it careered from side to side.

As suddenly as the nightmare began, it ended, and the shaken couple drew up at a coffee shop to calm their nerves.

It was while they were there that they realized two hours had mysteriously passed.

Later, Luli went to a hypnotist to try to fill in the gap in her memory.

'There are two small UFOs above us,' she said. 'I'm feeling sick, nauseated. Our car is being grabbed by the top. A light from the small ship is holding us. We're being held prisoner by this light. It's horrible.'

Her voice shook and her body was racked with sobs as she went on. 'We have entered the black disc from the bottom. The car is inside the UFO, but we are outside the car. They are putting a tube in my ear. There are tubes everywhere. They're pulling my hair!'

'They have huge horrible rat ears and their mouths are like slits. There are five of them, and their skin is grey and sticky.'

She described how she saw her friend lying unconscious on a table being examined by the aliens with a curious ray that reeked of sulphur.

When she and Fauze reached the coffee shop, they were so obviously shaken that the owner asked them what was wrong. When they told him what they had seen, he said, 'You're not the only ones to have had trouble on that road. One of my friends was chased by a UFO there.'

Maryland, 1973: Steven Kilburn, a student at Maryland University, claims he was abducted when driving along a quiet road one night. Under hypnosis he said, 'There are two lights in the sky going over the highway; over the trees I see a shadow of something. I'm coming down the hill and finally get to the spot where I think it will be and I pull over. I don't really want to go over there, but the car went to the right – it was real violent, as if it was being sucked along by a giant magnet.'

Steven watched dumbfounded as three figures approached his car. 'They were really strange,' he said later and, again under hypnosis, went on to say, 'They're small, below my shoulder. I see their faces and they're white, chalky, they look like they're made out of rubber. There's one, he's the boss. His eyes are really shiny. They look black. I don't see any pupils. His head is not round, it's like an inverted teardrop. There is a nose like a tiny ridge and two little holes like little pinholes.'

Steven could do nothing to stop himself from getting out of the car and walking towards the aliens he described so vividly. After that his mind is blank.

The next thing he knew he was back in his car and he looked

at his watch. He thought it could only be a few moments later, but he was aghast to find that three hours had passed.

A student hoax?

Experts who have talked to Steven and listened to tapes of what he said under hypnosis don't think so. They believe there was something menacing in Maryland that night in 1973.

Massachusetts, 1967: Betty Andreasson's story is one of the most extraordinary on record. Like most people who claim to have been abducted, her actual memory of the event is fragmentary and hazy, but under hypnosis it is as clear as crystal.

The year 1967 started badly for Betty. Her husband had been involved in a car crash and lay seriously injured in hospital some miles from South Ashburnham, the small New England town where the Andreassons lived.

To help Betty and her seven children, her parents had come to stay.

January 25th was a foggy night, and when the lights in the Andreasson house flickered and went out, Betty's father looked out of the window to see if there had been a power cut. Suddenly a pink light beamed through the window.

Gazing into the yard, the old man could hardly believe his eyes. As he testified later, 'The creatures I saw through the window of Betty's house were just like Hallowe'en freaks. I thought they had put on a funny kind of headdress imitating a moon man. The one in front looked at me and I felt kind of queer. That's all I knew.'

Then, according to Betty, while all the others in the house seemed to fall into a state of suspended animation, she saw an alien walk right in through a closed door! The creature was short, with grey skin and huge, slanting, catlike eyes. There were three fingers on each of its hands and it wore a shiny, figure-hugging uniform.

A voice in her head told Betty to follow it out into the yard. She had been chosen, the voice said, to help the world.

When she got outside, Betty saw more creatures crowding round an oval spaceship.

Once onboard, Betty was forced to undergo an embarrassing and painful medical examination. When it became obvious that she was in agony, the aliens put their hands on her forehead and the pain vanished.

The examination over, Betty was led through a long, black tunnel into a room where she was placed inside a glass globe.

Grey fluid flowed into the globe, seeping through Betty's clothes and into her skin.

'Don't be alarmed,' the voice in her head said. 'It will protect you as we travel to another world.'

Betty recalls more tunnels until eventually she was taken by two of the aliens from the spacecraft into a weird, seemingly lifeless landscape.

Surrounded by shimmering red lights, Betty and the aliens floated among plain, square buildings and it was then that she realized there were other creatures there – headless beings with lemur-like bodies.

The beasts terrified Betty, but she and the aliens passed safely among them into a green misty space in the middle of which was a pyramid encircled by a dazzling halo of floating crystals.

As they moved towards the light, Betty and the aliens found their path blocked by a huge eagle as tall as two men and giving off intense heat. Almost before Betty realized what she was looking at, the bird vanished and in its place the last flames of a dying fire flickered.

A new voice filled Betty's head. It told her she had been chosen for a mission that would be revealed to her in time.

Then the aliens took her back through the green mist and

past the headless creatures to the room where she had started.

The next thing she knew, Betty and one of the aliens were back in her misty yard in Massachusetts, and when she went into the house she found her parents and children in exactly the same state of suspended animation.

The alien with her led everyone up to their beds, and then left.

Next morning, Betty woke up thinking she had had a peculiar dream. She tried to forget about it, but vague fragments of it persisted. Eight years later, after she had read an article about UFOs and aliens, she contacted the investigators, who suggested hypnosis.

And that is when her extraordinary tale came out.

She was examined by psychiatrists who declared her absolutely sane. She was interrogated by experts who could offer no rational explanation for Betty's experience.

Her father swears that what little he remembers is true.

Her mission is still to be revealed to her, but Betty is waiting for the day when she will be told what she has to do to help the world.

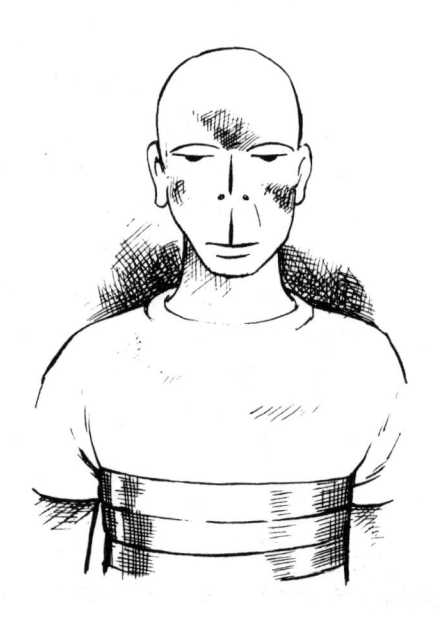

Mississippi, 1973: Charlie Hickson and his young friend Calvin Parker were out fishing from the pier that juts into the Shaupeter shipyard on the Pascagoula river one October evening.

Charlie was turning to get some bait from his box when he was startled by a sudden noise. Spinning round, he saw an egg-shaped object hovering just above the water. It was about 3 metres (10 feet) wide and 2.5 metres (8.2 feet) high.

Through the many flashing lights that almost dazzled him, he could just make out three creatures floating towards him. No door in the UFO had opened. One moment they weren't there, the next they were.

The ghostly creatures seemed to be about 1.5 metres (5 feet) tall, with wrinkled grey skin and pincer-like hands. Their large lipless mouths gaped wide below small pointed noses.

Both men swear that the aliens' legs didn't move as they drifted towards the pier.

Paralysed with fear, the two anglers could only sit and watch as the weird beings came closer and closer.

When they were within touching distance, one of the aliens reached out and ran a claw-like hand over Cal's brow. Cal instantly lapsed into unconsciousness and was carried towards the spacecraft by one alien.

A moment later, Charlie, still conscious, felt himself being lifted from the pier by the other two aliens.

His body felt numb and seemed to be weightless.

He then found himself in a room that glowed brightly although there was no obvious light source – he was just aware of a sensation of brightness.

As he looked round, he saw Cal being carried off into a room beyond.

Next he found himself quite literally hanging horizontally in the air, unable to move anything but his eyes.

Fear pulsed through him as a huge alien eye appeared from

nowhere and floated above his body, obviously scanning it. First his face, then his chest and the front of his legs were thoroughly examined by the menacing eye. The aliens then turned him face downwards, and he could almost feel the eye run over his back from head to toe.

The examination over, Charlie was turned over again, and out of the corner of his eye he saw a still-unconscious Cal drift towards him. Then suddenly they were both floating out of the spacecraft, across the water and onto the pier.

Charlie was on his feet for just a moment before his knees buckled under him and he slumped helplessly beside Cal's inert body.

Out over the water, the spaceship seemed to dissolve right before his eyes.

Next day at the sheriff's office, disbelieving lawmen questioned the two men for hours but they stuck to their story so convincingly that Captain Glen Ryder later said that if they had been lying, 'they should be in Hollywood'.

Unknown to the two men, the sheriff taped the interviews and when he left them alone, he allowed the tape to keep running.

When he played it back, 'expecting to hear the two men unthinkingly give themselves away, he was disappointed.

When the tape was replayed, Charlie and Cal's distressed voices could be heard talking about their experience. And at one point when Charlie left the room to go to the lavatory, Cal started to pray, pleading with his God to let him wake up and find it had all been a bad dream, for although he had no conscious recollection of what had happened in the spacecraft, he remembered his terror when he had seen the spaceship appear and the aliens advance towards him.

The day after their interrogation, Charlie and Cal were taken to the nearby Kessler air base where doctors checked them for signs of radiation contamination.

The tests were negative.

Not surprisingly, the story spread and Charlie and Cal were interviewed by the Mississippi Press . 'They were like robots,' Charlie said of the aliens. 'They acted like they had a specific thing to do, and they went ahead and did it. They didn't try to communicate with us and I know somehow they didn't intend to hurt us physically. But I feared they were going to take us away. I would like to emphasize that they didn't mean us any harm.'

Three days after their hair-raising experience, Cal and Charlie were interrogated again, this time by Dr J. Allen Hynek, then the leading expert in UFOs and aliens, and hypnotist, Dr James Harder.

Afterwards, Dr Hynek said he had no doubt that the two men had had a very terrifying experience. Dr Harder agreed. 'The experience they underwent was indeed a real one. A very strong feeling of terror is impossible to fake under hypnosis. And these men were terrified.'

The same can be said of the Methodist minister from Hartwell, Georgia, 700 kilometres (450 miles) away, when a UFO landed in front of his car on the same evening Charlie and Cal were taken aboard the alien spacecraft at the Shaupeter shipyard.

And shortly afterwards in Falkville, Alabama, Police Chief Greenhaw was called out by a woman who reported that a spaceship had landed in a field close to her house.

Greenhaw rushed to the spot, but found nothing.

However, as he drove home down a side road, a figure clad in silver stepped right out in front of his car. The policeman grabbed his camera and took four polaroid shots of the alien, who ran off as soon as it appeared to realize it was being photographed.

Chief Greenhaw got back in to his car and tried to catch up with the creature, but it had vanished.

Three alien sightings by reputable observers and one abduction took place at much the same time and in the same part of the world. Could they all have been figments of the imagination?

New Hampshire, 1961: It was September 17th and Betty Hill and her husband Barney were on their way home to New Jersey after spending a holiday in Canada. Barney was driving fast. There had been a hurricane alert for the East Coast and he was anxious to get home before the storm broke.

As they sped along Highway 3 through the White Mountains, they saw a bright light ahead.

'Probably an aircraft,' said Barney, 'or maybe a satellite.'

Betty was sure it was neither, and as they got closer to the light, she had an uneasy feeling that it was somehow tracking the car.

As they drove along a stretch of road known as Indian Head,

just outside the town of Lancaster, Betty persuaded Barney to slow down and, peering through the windscreen, they both tried to make out the source of the light.

Barney finally pulled over and switched off the engine.

'Where are you going?' asked Betty, as Barney leaned over and took his binoculars off the back seat.

'To take a closer look at that light,' replied Barney.

Betty watched anxiously as her husband got out of the car, walked towards the light and raised his binoculars.

In next to no time Barney was racing back to the car, and before Betty could open her mouth, he had switched on the ignition, pressed his foot on the accelerator and the car shot off in a cloud of dust.

He didn't say a word until they reached home.

There Barney told Betty what he had seen through his binoculars. The light, he said, was streaming out from a disc-shaped craft. Round the craft was a row of windows and through them curious creatures that made his hair stand on end with fright were staring out at him. He had waited no longer.

Betty was quick to report the incident to a local UFO expert, and when he called to ask for more details and take them through their terrifying experience once more, a frightening fact emerged. The Hills had lost two hours of their lives that night.

Betty started having nightmares so horrible that she would wake up screaming and dripping with sweat.

These nightmares persisted, and finally she got in touch with a doctor in Boston. He suggested hypnotism to find out the cause of her horrific dreams.

The hypnotist found it hard to believe Betty's story. But when Barney too agreed to be hypnotized, he corroborated everything she had said.

Barney had stopped the car, not to go and investigate the

light, but because the road ahead was blocked by small, silver-clad creatures with pear-shaped bald heads.

Next, Barney and Betty had been wafted out of their car into the aliens' spacecraft, where they were both subjected to a medical examination by the little aliens.

Betty's sleeves had been rolled up by the creatures, and pictures taken of her skin. One alien then scraped off flakes of her skin; another took samples of her hair and nails.

Betty was then told to lie flat on a table while a cluster of needles attached to wires was run over her body.

It was what followed that haunted Betty's dreams. As she lay on the table surrounded by the strange beings, one of them inserted a long needle into her navel.

The pain was terrible until one of the aliens rubbed his hands in front of her eyes, and it instantly evaporated.

The aliens seemed to be able to communicate with the Hills by telepathy, and after Betty was shown a map of the stars on which were indicated the aliens' routes through space, the Hills found themselves back in their car.

Then the sky glowed orange as the UFO sped off.

Neither Betty nor Barney could remember anything of what they had revealed when hypnotised though Betty admitted that the experience was reminiscent of her nightmares.

US Air Force records show that radar at Pease air force base not far from where the incident happened tracked an unidentified object in the early hours of September 19, 1961, so Betty and Barney may well have seen a UFO.

But were they whisked aboard and examined by little silver men?

They were hypnotized several more times and each time their story was the same. But some experts believe that Betty would obviously have told Barney about her nightmares and he may simply have repeated the story while in a trance.

Under hypnosis, Betty drew the star map shown to her by

the aliens. When it was examined by one expert, he pronounced it to be a star system called Zeta Reticula, 3.7 light years from the Earth, but another expert disagreed.

Barney died in 1969, convinced that he and his wife had been abducted by aliens.

And Betty? She firmly believes that what she said under hypnosis actually happened. Many believed her, but then when she began to report more and more encounters with the aliens from Zeta Reticula, people began to wonder if she had not made the whole thing up.

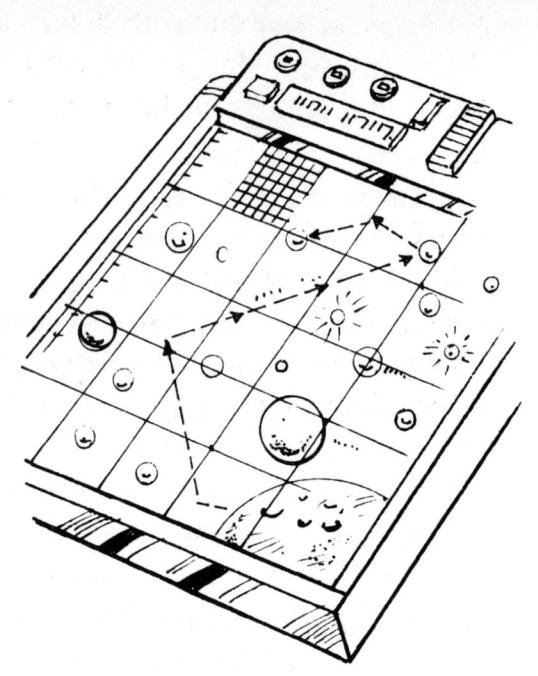

New York, 1989: Linda Cortile knew there was something wrong. At first she could not put her finger on what it was, but gradually she began to realise that at some time in the past she had been abducted by aliens. The more she thought about it, the more certain she became, and in April 1989 she contacted Manhattan ufologist Budd Hopkins.

Budd suggested hypnotism, and under its influence, Linda spoke of a day twenty years before when she had been taken aboard an alien spacecraft.

Eight months later she was back in Budd's rooms, telling him she thought she had been abducted again and asking to be hypnotized.

When Budd asked her what made her so sure, she told him that on November 30th she had woken up at around three o'clock in the morning feeling numb with fear. Certain that there was someone in the house, she tried to rouse her husband in bed beside her, but no matter how hard she shook him or how loudly she called his name, he didn't stir.

Suddenly the bedroom door opened and a spooky little alien was framed in the doorway.

At first, paralysed with fear, Linda somehow found the strength to pick up a pillow and throw it at the alien, who by now was creeping steadily towards her.

The pillow missed its target, and as the alien advanced, Linda's mind went blank.

The next thing she knew, she was again lying on her bed, alongside her sleeping husband.

Panic-stricken, she threw off the sheet and raced into her children's bedroom, terrified that something dreadful might have happened to them. The two boys were lying quite motionless and for a second Linda thought they were not breathing. But when she held a mirror to their faces, she was relieved to see it misting over.

Budd, an experienced ufologist, had heard many curious stories before, but none so weird as Linda's.

In a hypnotic trance, Linda revealed that there had not been just one alien in the apartment that night. There were four of them, each with large insect-like eyes that shone frighteningly from their dome-shaped heads.

Linda was powerless as they crept towards her bed. Then she felt herself being lifted up, and the next thing she knew she was floating up right through the closed window and into the cold night air, trapped in a beam of blue light.

Surrounded by the four aliens, she drifted towards their waiting spacecraft.

As soon as she was inside, she was given a thorough and frightening medical examination by the aliens before finding herself back in bed.

Budd reassured Linda that her experience was not unique; he had heard many such tales before. He asked her to get in touch with him again if she had any more alien contact, wrote up his case notes and, as the months passed, gradually forgot about Linda's abduction.

But in 1991 it was brought back to him with a jolt. When he opened his mail one morning he found a letter from two policemen who claimed that on the night of November 30th 1989, they had been escorting a VIP to a heliport in New York. As they drove across Brooklyn Bridge, the car's engine suddenly cut out.

The letter went on to say that something overhead had caught their attention, and looking up they had seen a woman in a white nightgown surrounded by four elfin-like creatures floating through the air towards a flying saucer!

As soon as the group were inside the craft, the UFO had shot off towards the East River.

Budd was unable to contact the two policemen as they had signed their letter using only their first names, but some time later he received another letter, this one from a woman who also claimed to have seen a white-clad figure accompanied by four aliens vanish into a UFO.

Budd got in touch with the writer, who confirmed that she too had been driving across Brooklyn Bridge on the same November night when her car had broken down for no apparent reason.

As she looked around her, she saw that the lights on the bridge were out and that all the other cars had come to a halt. It was only when she got out of her car to see what was wrong that she had spotted the ghostly figures overhead.

Of course, there are many questions that remain unanswered about Linda Cortile's abduction.

Her apartment is just across the street from the New York Post's Manhattan offices. Even at that time of night, or strictly speaking, early hours of the morning, the offices are busy. Why did no one working there ever come forward to report seeing anything untoward?

Who was the VIP being driven to the heliport? There is no record of anyone famous being on the bridge that night.

Why did the two policemen not sign their full names?

Why did they and the other witness wait for so long before coming forward? And why did no one else on Brooklyn Bridge report a power failure?

Despite that, Budd is certain that what Linda revealed under hypnosis actually happened and is equally certain that one day he will be proved right.

Peru, 1967: When Ludwig E. Pallman's body became racked with pain and his temperature shot up, he was rushed to the Maison Française Hospital in Lima where doctors found he was suffering from acute kidney problems.

Two years previously, when Ludwig was in India on a business trip, he had made friends with an Indian called Satu Ra. After three or four weeks, during which time Satu Ra introduced him to his family, he confessed to Ludwig that he and the others were actually ExtraTerrestrials.

Ludwig thought that his new friend was joking, but when Satu Ra suggested beaming him up to his spacecraft, he laughingly agreed.

He wasn't laughing a few moments later when he found himself inside a UFO, looking down on the world far below.

After a few hours he was beamed back to Earth, and a day or two later bade farewell to his alien friend.

Then, years later, he was rushed to hospital where he was told that he had to have an operation.

Ludwig's operation was to be performed the day after he had been diagnosed with a serious kidney condition.

That night Ludwig woke up to find that he was not alone. He had a visitor whom he immediately recognized as Xita, Satu Ra's sister.

Very gently she massaged his body, then handed him a pill to take.

As soon as he had swallowed it, Xita disappeared – simply vanished into thin air.

Almost immediately Ludwig felt his pain evaporate, and when his fever broke, he fell into a deep sleep.

The next morning when nurses came to prepare him for his operation, they were astonished to find their patient sitting up in bed and asking for breakfast.

Doctors examined him, found his kidneys were in good working order and his temperature absolutely normal. He was in perfect health.

'You're as fit as a flea,' one of the doctors said. 'Yesterday you were a very sick man, but today you are a different person.'

The medical team were naturally sceptical when Ludwig told them that during the night he had had a close encounter of the fourth kind with a friendly alien who had cured him.

But sceptical or not, they had no explanation to offer for his miraculous recovery.

And anyone who refuses to believe this story can contact the hospital where Ludwig E. Pallman's case is on the records.

Scotland, 1979: Bob Taylor, a fifty-year-old father of seven grown-up children, was not abducted by aliens. But if his story is true, it was a close-run thing.

Bob was walking his dog in the tree-clad hills near his home in West Lothian early one Friday morning in November. As he approached a clearing in the woods, a strong, acrid smell filled his nostrils.

His red setter, usually a placid pet, started to bark loudly and refused to go further. Bob peered into the clearing.

In the middle sat a machine shaped like a spacecraft. But before he could move closer two creatures stepped from it.

Bob was transfixed by what he later described as two wheels with arms attached which approached him, slowly at first, then suddenly darting forward and grabbing him round the legs.

Bob tried to fight them off, but as he struggled, the world went black and he lost consciousness.

When he came to, the aliens and the spacecraft had vanished. He was lying on his back in the middle of the clearing, his trousers ripped and his legs badly scratched and bleeding.

He ran back to his van which he had left at the edge of the woods, but when he switched the engine on and rammed it into gear, the wheels turned uselessly, sending up showers of mud behind them and not moving forward by as much as a centimetre.

Abandoning the useless vehicle, Bob staggered the 2.4 kilometre (1.5 miles) to his home, vague memories of being pulled towards the spacecraft flooding his head as he stumbled through the undergrowth with his still terrified dog at his heels.

When the police went to investigate, they found Bob's stranded van, the engine still chugging. In the clearing there were deep triangular marks on the ground that could have been made by a machine, and also two parallel ruts that might have been caused by someone being dragged.

The police weren't the only ones to check the clearing.

Later that day, Malcolm Drummond, Bob's boss at the Livingstone Development Corporation, went to have a look.

Like the police, Malcolm was intrigued by the marks that might have been made by the legs of a machine. 'Bob Taylor,' he said, 'is not a man to make something up. If he says he was attacked by some creatures, then there must have been something there.'

Val D'Oise, France, 1979: Nineteen-year-old Frenchman Frank Fontaine was enjoying life. He was happily married, the father of a lovely six-month old baby, and the business he had started with two friends was beginning to do well.

It was early one November morning and Frank and his partners were loading clothes into their van for the market at Gisors, a small town halfway between Paris and Rouen. Suddenly they heard a noise overhead and, looking up, they saw a bright revolving light.

Frank's friends, Jean-Pierre Prevot and Saloman N'diaye, ran indoors to get a camera, but rather than wait for them, Frank started up the van and drove off to the spot where the UFO looked as if it would land.

Later, Jean-Pierre told the police that when he and Saloman returned, the van was about 200 metres (630 feet away), encircled by a halo of bright light. Close by, three more lights were shining brightly. As they watched, the lights converged on their target – the van.

Slowly the halo rose up. Jean-Pierre and Saloman ran to the van. The engine was running, the door was open, but there was no sign of Frank.

Astounded and frightened, the two men ran to the nearest gendarmerie to report what had happened.

At first, the officers scoffed at their tale, but Jean-Pierre and

Saloman swore they were telling the truth and insisted that what they described had actually happened.

The police talked to the young men's families who vouched for the lads' honesty and trustworthiness.

The pair then gladly agreed to be tested for alcohol and drugs. There was not a trace of either in their bodies.

The van was tested for traces of radiation. There were none.

The police checked with air bases all over France to find out if there had been reports of UFO sightings that day. Again they drew a blank.

Photographs of Frank Fontaine were circulated to police stations around the country. But no one had seen him.

One week later, at almost exactly the same time of Frank's disappearance, Saloman was roused from sleep by a knock on his door. When he opened it, Frank stood there on the doorstep.

He told Saloman that he had found himself somehow returned to the spot where the van had stood the previous week.

'What's happened to it?' he asked. 'Has it been stolen?'

'What are you talking about?' asked Saloman. 'Where have you been for the last week?'

'What are you talking about?' said Frank. 'A week?'

'Do you know what day it is?' Saloman said.

'Monday, November the twenty-sixth.'

Saloman shook his head. 'It's Monday, all right,' he told his friend. 'But it's December the third. Frank, you've been missing for a week!'

The two men telephoned Jean-Pierre, and later all three went to the gendarmerie to report Frank's safe return.

If the police were glad to see him, they didn't say so. They interrogated Frank for hours, accusing him of playing a prank that had wasted a great deal of police time.

Frank denied this over and over again, but was quite unable

to tell the police where he had been. All that he could recall was driving towards the light, which had then landed like a tennis ball on the van's bonnet. As soon as it touched the van, Frank's eyes had started to smart, then everything went blank.

He told no story of being abducted by little green men, no tale of being whisked away on a flying saucer.

But if it wasn't a prank and the three Frenchmen were telling the truth, had Frank really been in the power of aliens? It is a serious possibility.

West Yorkshire, 1980: No one will ever know if Zygmunt Adamski really did have a Close Encounter of the Fourth Kind, for he did not live to tell his tale!

Zygmunt was a quiet man who had fled his native country when German troops marched into Poland in 1939. Once in Britain, he became a miner in the West Yorkshire coalfields and eventually settled in a peaceful suburb of Leeds, the largest city in the area.

On June 11th, 1980, telling his wife he would not be long, he left the house to buy a bag of potatoes. He was never seen again.

Five days later, his body was found in a coalyard in Todmorden, a small town 48 kilometres (30 miles) from his home.

Zygmunt had no connection with Todmorden and his devastated wife could offer no explanation as to why her husband should have gone there.

The police were puzzled and even after the inquest several questions remained unanswered.

Zygmunt's body was not found until five days after he disappeared. Where had he been for that time?

The young man who found the body swore under oath that it had not been there when he opened the coalyard that morning. How had it got there and who had put it there?

And why had parts of the body been burned by a corrosive substance that experts could not identify?

A doctor giving evidence at the inquest said that the victim had died following a heart attack, and that a corrosive substance had been carefully applied to the scalp, neck and back of the head, leaving the face and clothes untouched.

The coroner declared that it was quite the most mysterious death he had ever investigated, and postponed the hearing for three months to allow the police to continue their inquiries.

These inquiries added an astonishing new dimension to the case, one that first raised the possibility that Zygmunt Adamski might have died during a close encounter of the fourth kind.

One of the first policemen to reach the coalyard after the body had been discovered, PC Alan Godfrey, revealed that shortly afterwards, when he was driving through a housing estate in Todmorden, he had seen what he at first thought was a bus.

But when he realized the 'bus' was floating some 1.6 metres (5 feet) above the ground, he felt certain that he was looking at a UFO. The bottom part of the craft was spinning round and round, and above were rows of windows.

PC Godfrey tried to contact his station, but both his radio and his walkie-talkie were dead. Taking his notebook and pencil from his pocket, he started to sketch the UFO. By the time he finished, it had gone.

The astonished policeman, scared of being laughed at, decided not to tell anyone, but when he heard later that four policemen in nearby Halifax had reported seeing a UFO, he told his superiors what he had seen.

When UFO experts heard about the sighting they talked to PC Godfrey and learned that there had been some fifteen minutes between the time he had first seen the UFO to the time he finished the sketch that he couldn't account for.

The policeman agreed to be hypnotized and an astonishing story was revealed.

As he watched the UFO, Godfrey had suddenly been blinded by a dazzling light. When it faded, he found himself in a room with a tall, bearded figure wearing a skull cap. Somehow he knew was the figure was called Joseph.

A reporter who saw the video recording of the hypnosis session tells what happened next. 'He started crying, "They're horrible . . . small, three to four feet, like five-year-old lads. They have hands and heads like lamps. They keep touching me . . . They are making noises. They are robots! They're not human, they're robots. They're his. They're Joseph's. There's a dog. It's horrible!"'

By then PC Godfrey was thrashing around so wildly that the hypnotist called him out of his trance.

Later he was hypnotized again and this time spoke of being examined by a large machine. When the hypnotist asked him what it looked like, he cried, 'I must not answer that. I must not tell you. Each time I think about it, I get a pain.'

He concluded his story by saying that after the aliens had taken off his shoes and socks to examine his toes, he found himself back in his car.

PC Godfrey was a young, healthy officer.

Zygmunt was a fifty-six-year-old man whose health had been affected by his years working down the mines.

Could it be that the Polish ex-miner had been abducted by the same aliens who took PC Godfrey aboard?

Had Zygmunt died while he was being examined? Had he then been taken to the coalyard at Todmorden? Some people believe this to have happened.

Even the coroner was open to the suggestion. When eventually he made his report, he said that while his lawyer's mind told him there must be a simple explanation for

Zygmunt's death, 'I do admit that the failure of scientists to identify the corrosive substance which caused Mr Adamski's burns could lend some weight to the UFO theory. As a coroner, I cannot speculate, but I must admit that if I was walking on Ilkley Moor tomorrow and a UFO came down, I would not be surprised. I would be terrified, but not surprised.'

EYEWITNESS

The man who made the following sworn statement has asked to remain anonymous.

I was contacted late one night, eleven years ago, while working late to finish a printing job. Like most intelligent beings I was interested and curious [about UFOs and aliens] but had no expectation of a contact. They came to my shop door, insisted on my opening it, came in, looked around a bit, spoke no word, motioned me to come outside. As I did so I became aware of a large object a few metres overhead.

I was taken aboard and had my first experience of positive telepathy, a very informative few minutes. They left saying they would return soon. They kept their word . . . I think I can honestly say they returned a few hundred times in the past eleven years.

They have requested that I act as their physical earth-man contact with quite a number of our national and religious leaders.

Among their own people they use thought only, but they have learned to speak our language so perfectly that if one of them was to speak to you, you would not recognize him from one of your own people.

SPOOK FILES ENCYCLOPAEDIA

HAVE YOU BEEN ABDUCTED?

Most people who have been abducted forget about their experience which only gradually comes back to them, often under hypnosis. Maybe you have been whisked up into a spacecraft by aliens and your brain has blanked the abduction from your memory. Here are a few tell-tale signs:

Can't remember where you were for an hour or two? Many abductees report looking at their watches and being shocked when they realize that a period of time has elapsed they cannot account for, no matter how hard they think.

Curious mental pictures? When they try to fill in the missing hours, people who have been abducted find their minds filled with image after image that have absolutely no logical relationship with each other.

Dreamed of aliens lately? If you dream about little grey men with black, almond-shaped eyes, or other alien forms, maybe it's your subconscious trying to tell you what really happened. Vivid dreams about aliens are commonly experienced by abductees.

Can't sleep at night? Could be your body's way of stopping you recalling your terrifying experience in your dreams.

Had a nose bleed recently? Several abductees find that their noses start to bleed a day or two after they realize they have lost time and that the nose bleeds continue on and off until the abduction is recalled from the depths of their memories.

Can't remember how you got that scar? Maybe you were a patient in an alien operating theatre. Many men and women who claim to have been abducted were operated on by the alien kidnappers.

If you've answered 'Yes' to these questions, who knows, you could have been taken aboard an alien spacecraft and don't remember anything about it. Yet!

TEN PEOPLE WHO HAVE BEEN CURED BY ALIENS

Olga Adler was lying in bed one day in 1973, almost unable to move because of chronic back pain.

Through her closed eyes, the American woman suddenly became conscious that the room had become much brighter, and when she opened her eyes, she was astonished, but not at all afraid, to see a monk-like figure, its face hidden in the folds of his hood, moving towards her.

'In his arms he held what looked like a heavy metal cylinder. He put it behind my back as I lay there on my side, and pressed it down,' Olga said later. 'I could feel the bed depress with the extra weight and could see the figure leaning on it directly, the face always in deep shadow.'

Olga felt what she described as a 'comfortable warmth' penetrate her body, which started to tingle.

For five minutes the figure held the cylinder at Olga's back, while she enjoyed its soothing waves. Then the spectre, cylinder in hand, moved slowly towards the closed bedroom door and vanished right through it.

Now thoroughly relaxed, Olga fell into a deep sleep, and when she awoke, her back pain was gone. She could bend, she could twist, thanks to a Close Encounter of a very beneficial kind.

Beth Collings was driving along a Virginia highway in December 1992 when she saw what she later described as a low flying aircraft overhead.

Suddenly the engine cut out and the car came to a halt on the lonely road.

As she sat there, turning the ignition key over and over again to try and restart the engine, a bright light shot out from whatever was hovering in the air just in front of her and caught the car in its glare.

For a moment Beth sat there, frozen to her seat, before turning the key once more. Relief flooded through her as the engine roared into life and she shot off down the road.

It was only when she got home that she realized her frozen moment had lasted for half-an-hour, and it was only when she was getting ready for bed that she noticed that her contact lenses were missing.

'I certainly had them on when I got into the car,' she said when she related the story to her optician, who was astonished to find that his previously short-sighted patient now had perfect vision!

Carl Higdon had been suffering on and off from painful kidney stones for some time and felt a warning twinge one day in 1976 when he was out hunting in Medicine Bow National Forest in Wyoming.

Even so, he was delighted when he spotted some elk within range. He raised his gun, took aim and fired.

Carl was a good shot and expected the elk he had had in his sights to fall down dead on the ground.

Imagine his astonishment when the bullet floated gently from his rifle and fell to earth about 15 metres (49 feet) away.

Looking round, Carl saw he was not alone. Standing a little way off, he saw something he immediately knew was an alien. 1.8 metres (6 feet) tall, with yellowish skin, a head that grew straight from its shoulders, straw coloured hair from which two antennae grew. The strange creature was wearing a one-piece jumpsuit.

Carl felt no fear as the alien walked towards him.

When the two were arm's length from each other, Carl noticed that the alien was holding some pills in the palm of his hand. A voice in his head told him he should take one and swallow it, which he did.

The twinges of pain vanished, and from that day on Carl Higdon has never been bothered by kidney stones again.

Robert W Goode, a Texan patrol deputy, was a passenger in a car with his friend chief-deputy Billy McCoy, who was at the wheel. It was September 3rd, 1965, and the two men were keen to get home after watching a high-school football game.

Robert was nursing a painfully throbbing finger, having been bitten by his son's pet baby alligator.

Suddenly, without warning, Billy pulled the car off the road.

Robert was just about to ask him why when he saw strange lights beaming skywards from the right side of the road.

As the two men watched, the lights moved towards them and as they got closer and closer, they saw an enormous UFO floating in the sky above.

Suddenly the inside of the car was bathed in light and Robert felt a rush of warm air on his left arm, which was hanging out the car window.

'Let's get out of here,' Billy cried, pressing his foot down hard on the accelerator.

As the car roared down the highway, Robert realized that his injured finger had stopped throbbing. He pulled off the bandage and was astounded to see that there was no sign of the wound.

If Robert was astonished, so was his doctor when she examined his finger the next day. There was not a trace of scar tissue on a damaged finger which only two days before she herself had bathed and bandaged.

Morgana van Klausen went to her doctor on December 4th, 1994, because she was feeling feverish. She expected to be given a prescription and told to go home and stay in bed for a day or two until the fever had passed.

But after a thorough examination, Morgana's physician told her she had a cyst that would require surgery as soon as possible.

The operation was scheduled to take place on December 14th, to give Morgana time to recover from her fever.

The day before she was due to go into hospital, Morgana was out driving with her son when they saw a white, triangular-shaped craft hovering nearby.

They were able to watch it for a moment or two before it sped off.

It was then that her son turned to Morgana and said, 'Mom! This is a good sign. They are protecting us. You wait and see, you'll have no more problems.'

'Someone up there likes me,' Morgana laughed.

That evening, after she had finished packing her bag to take to hospital and gone to bed, Morgana was overcome by an intense pain in the area where she knew the cyst to be.

She tried to get out of bed, but the pain was so severe that she couldn't move, and moments later she passed out.

When she awoke the next morning the pain was gone, but still she set off for the hospital.

'We'll just take another couple of X-rays,' she was told as she lay on her bed, 'to make sure your cyst hasn't got any bigger.'

The doctors, surgeons and nurses all crowded around the new X-rays once they had been processed.

Fearing the worst, Morgana asked if the cyst had grown much bigger, and whether the surgery would be more extensive than had been planned.

But the medical team

shook their heads. The cyst had vanished completely.

The old X-rays were studied and the cyst was clearly there for all to see.

Morgana and her son had been right. Someone up there liked her.

Eduard Meier swears that when he was suffering from pneumonia in 1978, he was taken aboard a UFO where human-like aliens cured him. One of them, Sfath, told Eduard this was not first time they had met.

Eduard had no recollection of meeting an alien before, but that was hardly surprising as their previous encounter had been when Eduard was only six months old.

Sfath told Eduard that when he was a baby in 1937, he had contracted pneumonia and had been expected to die.

It was Sfath who had cured him.

When Eduard asked his mother about this, she confirmed what Sfath had told him.

When at the age of 41 he confounded all expectations and lived through another bout of pnuemonia, all the doctors could do was shake their heads and talk about a miracle!

Richard T (an alien contactee who prefers that his full name is not revealed) had been confined to a wheelchair since a grave illness had left him paralysed. He was able to drive a specially adapted van and enjoyed getting out of the house as often as he could.

One day he drove himself to a beach close to his Californian home and was enjoying watching people at play when he looked up and saw a torpedo-shaped UFO in the sky above.

No one else on the beach seemed to have noticed it, for they all carried on as normal.

The next thing Richard knew, he found himself inside the UFO, surrounded by small human-like aliens with disproportionately large heads and large, almond-shaped eyes. He felt no fear, just wave after wave of calm washing over him, making him feel pleasantly sleepy.

When he came to, he was somehow back in his van with his wheelchair folded up beside him. He drove home, manoeuvred the chair onto the pavement as usual and was about to swing his body into it, when he felt an odd sensation in his legs.

Even so, he got into the chair and wheeled himself into the house.

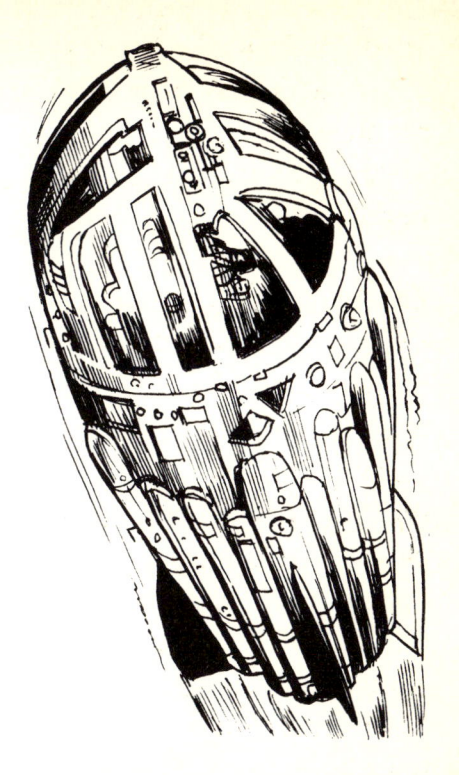

Over the next few weeks his paralysis gradually eased, and it wasn't long before he was able to walk, albeit with the aid of a cane.

Robert's doctors were astonished, not just at his 'cure' but at his conviction that it had been the aliens he met at the beach who had brought it about.

Richard Rylka has been cured by aliens, not just once, but on several occasions!

The first time was when he was a child, growing up in New Jersey in the early 1950s. After a heavy snowfall, Richard was out sledging with some friends, when, unable to steer his sleigh, he careered out of control down a hill into the path of an oncoming car.

The unfortunate boy was knocked unconscious and thrown off his sledge into a deep snowdrift.

Although he lay there for only a few minutes while the ambulance was called, the freezing temperature affected one of his ears, and when the first-aid men arrived on the scene, Richard was hardly able to hear what they said to him.

Richard was taken to hospital, thoroughly examined and after his cuts had been bandaged and his bruised limbs strapped up, was left alone to try to get some sleep. As he lay there in the darkened ward, he was surprised when two figures he instantly knew to be aliens entered the big room.

Words somehow transmitted telepathically into his head told him that they were called Koran and Nepos and that they had come to help him.

Beams of healing energy flooded from Koran and Nepos, and all Richard's pain evaporated away.

His hearing remained impaired for some time afterwards, but was eventually restored after the infection that had caused it was treated with penicillin, then still a new drug.

Some years later, in the 1960s, Richard, by now a young man, was working for a medical firm in New Jersey, USA.

One day he was operating a piece of heavy equipment called a drum-lifter when his index finger became caught in the hydraulic machinery.

His friends rushed to help him, but by the time they managed to switch off the machine, Richard's finger was numb and paralysed, white and horribly mangled.

The company's nurse took one look at the mutilated finger and called a cab to rush him to the Middlesex General Hospital in nearby Brunswick, N.J. There, after wrapping his finger in an ice-pack, a doctor went to fetch a mobile X-ray machine, leaving him on his own in the emergency room.

Suddenly, who should appear but his old friends, Koran and Nepos.

The two aliens held their hands over Richard's injured finger, then vanished.

When the doctor returned, he found no sign of the injury, and although the finger remained numb for several months, Richard was back at work within days of his accident.

Richard Rylka seems to have been dogged by accidents, for in 1970 he was involved in a dreadful car crash.

As he hovered between life and death, Koran and Nepos appeared yet again, telling him that he was so badly injured he should, by rights, be dead. But they promised to heal him, and true to their word, Richard was soon back on his feet.

Cynics scoffed, of course, when Richard told them of these and at least two other occasions when he was cured by aliens, but he is quite adamant that had it not been for Koran and Nepos, he would probably be dead by now.

Bert Twiggs, from Hubbard, Oregon, was in bed with a dreadful cold on July 14th, 1989. His wife, Denise, begged him to go and see the doctor, but Bert refused and only after Denise insisted did he promise her that he would go the next day if he was no better.

As the day wore on, Bert's cough worsened, his breathing became more and more laboured and his stomach began to hurt.

In the middle of the night, both Denise and Bert woke up with a start.

'I've just had the most amazing dream,' said Bert.

'So have I,' nodded Denise.

Husband and wife had experienced an identical dream in which a group of aliens from a planet in the Andromeda galaxy had come into the bedroom. They told Bert that they were concerned about his illness which, they said, was near fatal. They had come, they went on, to cure him.

After giving Bert an injection, they vanished and it was then that Bert and Denise had woken up, When they looked at Bert's arm, there was a clear needle mark in the exact spot where both had dreamed he had been given the alien injection.

By the next morning Bert's cold was much better, his breathing was normal and his stomach pains had gone.

And the day after that, he was completely cured.

Hector Vasquez of San Juan, Puerto Rico was jolted awake one night in August 1980 with severe pains in his side, which he knew were caused by his kidney stones troubling him again.

He realized he had to get to hospital, so he sent one of his children to ask his friend David Delmundo, a Baptist minister, to drive him there.

On the way to the hospital a luminous orange disc appeared in the dark sky and hovered just ahead of them for a minute or two before flying alongside for a while.

Next, it flew back in front of the car, making strange patterns as it moved.

Hector didn't see what was happening, because he was lying on the back seat, doubled up with pain and with his eyes closed. When David told him that a UFO was flying by them outside, Hector scoffed at him.

But when he looked out, he saw that his friend was telling the truth.

As they continued the journey to the hospital, the UFO floated round the car several times and then vanished, and by the time Hector and David reached the hospital, Hector's pain had gone.

Doctors who examined him found no trace of kidney stones, although according to their medical records, there should have been.

And from that day to this, Hector Vasquez has enjoyed a normal, pain-free life.

SPOOK FILES ENCYCLOPAEDIA

ANIMAL MUTILATIONS

One day in April, 1897, near the small town of Vernon in Kansas, a giant, cigar-shaped UFO was spotted hovering over a ranch belonging to former US congressman, Alexander Hamilton. Ten witnesses swear that they saw one of the strange creatures aboard lean out of a porthole, lasso a cow and haul it into the spacecraft.

The next day, the skin, head and legs of the abducted beast were found scattered in a nearby field.

This was the first case on record of animals being mutilated by aliens.

A subsequent investigation many years afterwards cast doubt on the story, but seventy years later the first case of modern animal mutilation was reported and since then there have been several outbreaks which defy explanation.

It was in September 1967 that the skinless body of a pony called Snippy was found in a field in Alamosa County, Colorado, following a spate of UFO sightings in the area. Fifteen small, circular scorch marks were found over an area of 4,500 square metres around the carcass, but there were no footprints to be seen, and Snippy's own hoofprints trailed off 30 metres from where he lay, not only flayed, but drained of blood, too.

There were small incisions cut into the dead flesh, obviously made by someone or something skilled in surgery, but there was not a drop of blood to be seen.

Over the next week or two, the carcasses of four cows and four more ponies were found in the area in almost identical circumstances.

Since then there have been outbreaks of unexplained animal mutilations in many parts of the United States - in Kansas and Pennsylvania later in 1967, the Midwest from 1975-6, and Colorado again in the early 1980s. The outbreaks are sometimes accompanied by an increase in reported UFO sightings, sometimes by unseasonably bad weather and sometimes by what has been described as, 'dancing lights' in the night sky.

During the Midwest outbreaks, the mutilated carcasses of farm animals were found in fifteen states, including South Dakota, Montana, New Mexico and Texas. In many places, mysterious, unmarked helicopters, often painted black, were reported to have buzzed round the areas where dead animals had either been found or were later discovered. Some ranchers became so worried by these helicopters that they took potshots at them with powerful rifles, yet no helicopter pilot filed a report that his or her aircraft had been shot at.

At one site in New Mexico, investigators found that one carcass had been daubed with fluorescent paint that showed up only under ultra-violet light.

A hoax? No one has ever admitted, even anonymously, to playing such a cruel trick and most hoaxers either eventually confess or are found out.

Predators? No predatory animals leaves its victim completely bloodless. No predators remove the victims' internal organs, tongues, eyes and ears and leave the rest untouched.

To add to the mystery, when samples of the body tissue of a mutilated calf were taken to a laboratory in Colorado for examination in 1981, someone, or something, broke in and stole them all, except for one small piece of hide. When it was examined, it was found that the incisions had been made with inhuman surgical skill, for whatever instrument had been used, it had cut between cells, not through them!

And even more curious, neither the hungriest coyote nor most ravenous dog would go within five metres of any of the animals that have been found mutilated during these outbreaks!

TEN FILMS ABOUT ALIENS

ALIEN
Ridley Scott's classic alien movie. Made in 1979, this terrifying tale of an alien munching its way through the crew of an earth-bound spaceship had audiences all over the world on the edge of their seats. The movie spawned three sequels, none of which matched the horror of the original.

CLOSE ENCOUNTERS OF THE THIRD KIND
1979 classic directed by movie maestro, Steven Spielberg. When an alien spacecraft lands in America, scientists find that the only way to communicate with the crew is musically. Hauntingly beautiful.

ET
Another Spielberg masterpiece in which a stranded little alien befriends a group of cute American kids who help him get home. Witty, warm and wonderful.

THE FIFTH ELEMENT
It's undercover agent, taxi-driving Bruce Willis to the rescue when evil alien Gary Oldman tries to destroy the world. Great fun, and very exciting. Directed by Luc Besson.

FLASH GORDON
1930s comic strip hero brought to the screen in glorious Technicolor in 1980 to save the Earth from one of the most evil of all aliens, Ming the Merciless. With Sam J Jones as Flash and Max von Sydow as Ming, Flash was great fun.

INDEPENDENCE DAY
Roland Americh's 1996 blockbuster that sees us under threat from aliens from the other side of the galaxy aiming to destroy the Earth. Just as well US President Whitmore is on hand to clamber into a jet fighter to lead a fleet of planes aiming to nuke the aliens out of existence.

MARS ATTACKS
A 1996 movie, with wonderful performances by Jack Nicholson, Glen Close and others, but all upstaged by the Martian Ambassador. He may say he comes in peace, but it's soon plain that he's lying through his teeth. Directed by Tim Burton.

MEN IN BLACK
1997 romp featuring Tommy Lee Jones and Will Smith working for a top-secret US agency dedicated to ridding the universe of alien scum. Directed by Barry Sonnfeld, MIB was one of the top box-office and video rentals of the second half of the 1990s.

STAR WARS
Three classic alien movies crammed with extraordinary characters from the evil Jabba the Hutt to the Wookie hero, Chewbacca. Directed by George Lucas, Star Wars: A New Hope (1977), The Empire Strikes Back (1980) and Return of the Jedi (1983), rank among the best sci-fi movies ever made.

STARSHIP TROOPERS
It's alien bugs versus the world in this action-packed 1997 box-office hit. Directed by Paul Verhoeven, the movie had them queuing in droves wherever it was shown.

SPOOK FILES ENCYCLOPAEDIA

TEN JOKES ABOUT ALIENS

What did the alien say to the chicken?
'Eggs-terminate'

Robot: 'My batteries have gone flat. Can you help me?'
Alien: 'Sure! But I'm going to have to charge you.'

'Doctor! Doctor! I keep thinking I'm a Martian.'
'Don't be silly. You're not from Mars. You're from Venus, just like me.'

Police officer: 'You're getting a speed ticket. You were doing at least 125 km/h in that spaceship. What's your name?'
Alien: 'Sprty Zohgytu My'retke Orbyzw.'
Police officer: 'On second thoughts, I'll let you off with a warning this time, but don't do it again.'

Alien 1: 'Where on Earth did your mother land her spaceship?'
Alien 2: 'Alaska!'
Alien 1: 'Never mind! I'll ask her myself!'

Alien: 'I wish you people on Earth could make up your mind about things.'
Earthling: 'What do you mean?'
Alien: 'I asked someone the time this morning. And now I've asked you and you've given me a completely different answer!'

Alien 1: 'If it wasn't for your orange stripes you would look just like my sister.'
Alien 2: 'I don't have orange stripes.'
Alien 1: 'I know you don't. But my sister has.'

Alien: 'An Earthling sandwich please.'
Alien Waiter: 'Sorry, Sir. No can do.'
Alien: 'You mean you don't serve Earthling sandwiches?'
Alien Waiter: 'Oh yes, Sir. But we're out of bread.'

Optician: 'Can you read the bottom line?'
Alien: 'Yup! ZLPRMOSQRIE'
Optician: 'Gosh! No one has ever read it so quickly before.'
Alien: 'Not surprised. Very few people live on ZLPRMOSQRIE.'

Spaceman 1: 'Why on Earth are you smearing yourself with apricot jam?'
Spaceman 2: 'It keep the aliens away.'
Spaceman 1: 'But we haven't seen any aliens on this planet.'
Spaceman 2: 'I know. See how well it works!'

SPOOK FILES ENCYCLOPAEDIA

TEN BOOKS TO READ ABOUT ALIENS AND UFOS

Alien Contact – The First Fifty Years
Jenny Randles (Collins & Brown, 1997)

The Alien World
Peter Brookesmith (editor) (Orbis Publishing, 1984)

Close Encounters of the Fourth Kind
C. D. Bryan (Weidenfeld, 1995)

The Complete Book of UFOs
Jenny Randles and Peter Hough (Piatkus, 1994)

Marvels and Mysteries – Aliens
(Orbis Publishing, 1997)

Marvels and Mysteries – UFOs
(Parragon, 1995)

Strange But True – Aliens
Damon Wilson (Parragon, 1997)

The UFO Encyclopaedia
John Spencer (Headline, 1991)

The World's Greatest UFO Mysteries
Roger Boar and Nigel Blundell (Octopus Books, 1983)

UFO, The Complete Sightings Catalogue
Peter Brookesmith (Blandford, 1995)

SPOOK FILES ENCYCLOPAEDIA

TEN ORGANIZATIONS TO CONTACT IF YOU SEE A UFO

Australian UFO Centre,
PO Box W42, West Pennant Hills, NSW 2125, Australia

British UFO Research Association,
BM BUFORA, London WC1N 3XX

Canada UFO Research Network,
PO Box 15, Station A, Willowdale, Ontario, M2N 5S7, Canada

J Allen Hynek Center for UFO Studies,
2457 West Peterson Avenue, Chicago, IL 60659, USA

Mutual UFOI Network,
103 Oldtown Road, Seguin, TX 78159-4099, USA

Northern Anomalies Research Organization,
6 Silsden Avenue, Lowton, Warrington, WA3 1UE

Ovni Presence,
SOS OVNI BP 324, 13611, Aix-en-Provence, Cedex 1, France

Scottish Mysteries Association,
35 Fountain Road, Bridge of Allen, Central Region, FK9 4AU

UFO Research Centre Canada,
Dept 25, 1665 Robson Street, Vancouver, British Columbia, V6G 362, Canada

Welsh Federation of UFOlogists,
PO Box 43, Rhyl, Clwyd, LL18 1YW

AND FINALLY

As well as Close Encounters of the First, Second, Third and Fourth kinds, there are also Close Encounters of the Fifth Kind, during which telepathy is used. They are rare and, frankly, not especially exciting.

So let's finish on a real mystery – a Close Encounter of a Truly Astonishing Kind . . .

Cock-fighting is illegal in Texas and has been for a long time. But that doesn't mean it never happens.

It was a summer's day in 1959 when thirteen-year-old Susan Neverez Morton and her sister and brother-in-law joined a crowd at a secret spot outside the small town of Pleasanton where illicit cock-fights were regularly held.

As Susan and the others squeezed onto the wooden benches placed in a circle round an open patch of ground, two cockerels were let out of their boxes by their proud owners.

The two birds strutted up to each other and struck out, their claws flashing in the afternoon sun. It wasn't long before both birds, weakened by loss of blood, were on the point of collapse.

Just as they both slumped to the ground, someone looked up and saw a large glowing object hovering over the makeshift stadium.

Suddenly, two beams of light flashed from the UFO and

bathed the two exhausted birds in its glow.

'It was amazing,' Susan said later. 'Their small, broken bodies glowed eerily for a few seconds. Then slowly they both got up on their little chicken feet and began strutting around with robust, healthy enthusiasm.'

After a few moments, the UFO changed colour from red to orange and streaked off at a speed that took the spectators' breath away.

Even now, all these years later, those who are still alive talk about the day they saw two apparently terminally injured birds rise from the near dead and squawk noisily at each other before being put back in their boxes by their astonished owners.

A Close Encounter Strictly for the Birds!

All The Spook Files titles are available from
> **Littlehampton Book Services,**
> **14 Eldon Way,**
> **Lineside Estate,**
> **Littlehampton,**
> **West Sussex**
> **BN17 7HE.**
> **Telephone: 01903 721596 Fax: 01903 828802**
> **e-mail: 100067.1631@compuserve.com**

Other titles include:

THE SPOOK FILES: THE MUMMY FROM MARS

Who wouldn't scream if they saw a 4000-year-old Egyptian mummy move? Carrie Potter certainly did.

Maybe she was just imagining it. After all, it was stiflingly hot in the museum – and the heat can do pretty strange things to a person's mind.

There was only one way to find out. But when Carrie and her twin brother, Phil, try to prove that she wasn't seeing things, it's not long before they're wishing they had left well alone . . .

ISBN: 0 233 99093 3   £2.99

THE SPOOK FILES: PRISONER OF TERROR

What starts out as a harmless piece of mischief looks sure to end in disaster for eleven-year-old Per Dawson when he's taken prisoner by aliens from another planet in a galaxy at the other side of the universe.

Can Per find the courage to face his worst nightmare and return to his own place and time, or is he doomed to be a prisoner of terror for the rest of his life?

ISBN: 0 233 99195 6   £2.99

THE SPOOK FILES: ALIEN ATTACK

There's no way that Damian Ross is going to miss the chance of watching a satellite launch from close up. Even if it means that he has to resort to a little blackmail to be there.

But Damian finds himself at the centre of a countdown to disaster when he sees something of an extremely alien nature just minutes before blast off . . .

. . . And unless he can make people believe him, the world is going to be a different place. A very different place!

ISBN: 0 233 99091 7   £2.99

THE SPOOK FILES: THE SWARM FROM OUTER SPACE

Looking back, it all started when Kelly Bascamb's cat was struck down with a mysterious illness. Only no one saw the danger until it looked as if it was too late and the world was doomed.

By then, an entire village was being held hostage by a band of aliens, guided through space by a swarm of killer bees from another world.

Can Kelly and one of her researchers destroy the swarm before it's too late, or will the main alien force land and take over the Earth?

ISBN: 0 233 99297 9   £2.99

THE SPOOK FILES: FIENDS FROM PLANET X

What eleven-year-old boy could keep his hands off the most brilliant PC he's ever seen – especially when it's in his mother's study?

Not Zak Hawkins. Even though it means risking a force-ten row if he's found out.

But what starts as a harmless piece of fun, ends up with the world on the brink of nuclear war. Thanks to Zak . . . and the red-eyed aliens, other there . . .
Somewhere!

ISBN: 0 233 99092 5   £2.99

THE SPOOK FILES: SCARECROW

City kid Josh Randolph hates his new life in the county. It's dull, dull, dull. He yearns for the buzz of the streets and the mates he left behind.

But when he is ensnared in a hair-raising struggle between aliens from another galaxy, he begins to realise that the country may not be so bad after all – if he ever gets back to it!

ISBN: 0 233 99194 8   £2.99

THE SPOOK FILES: UFO ATTACK

Twelve-year-old Tug Wilson's plans to escape from the detention centre have hardly got off the ground before he sees a UFO landing.

Within hours it's Tug and five of his ne'er-do-well companions against a group of aliens intent on colonising the Earth.

But even if Tug thwarts the evil creatures from deep space, will the Earth survive a second threat – a threat that could make the planet uninhabitable for thousands of years?

ISBN: 0 233 99292 8   £2.99

THE SPOOK FILES: THE ALIENS NEXT DOOR

There's something about Rosie's new neighbours that doesn't add up – something almost alien. And when she sees a UFO hovering above their house, she's convinced they're from another planet.

But there's another shock in store for Rosie and her friends – one that makes them believe they'll never see their parents again . . .

ISBN: 0 233 99193 X   £2.99

THE SPOOK FILES: CIRCUS OF FEAR

It's billed as the Greatest Show in the Universe – the most spectacular, the most thrilling circus there has even been.

But when top trapeze artists The Magnificent Magyars, are hired, it's not long before young Tomas Magyar and his friends realise that all is not what it seems in the big top.

In fact it's not long before they realise they are involved in a desperate struggle – a struggle which could leave them all dead at the hands of a band of aliens.

ISBN: 0 233 99203 0   £2.99

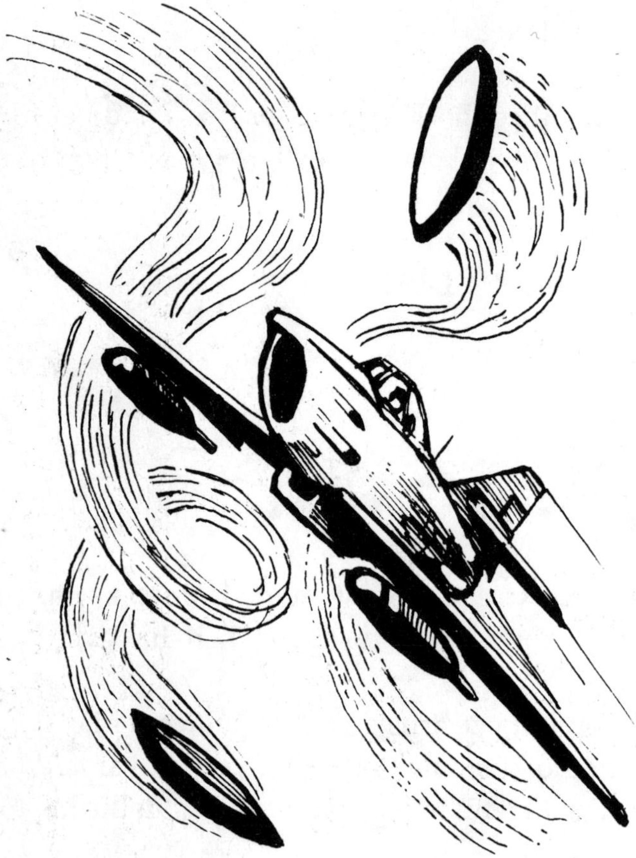